16.95

Margie Thompson
March 1994
bought in Seattle.
quilt-shopping with Lynn!

Pioneer Quiltmaker

The Story of Dorinda Moody Slade

1808~1895

Dorinda Slade.

Pioneer Quiltmaker

The Story of Dorinda Moody Slade 1808~1895

by Carolyn O'Bagy Davis

SANPETE PUBLICATIONS
Tucson, Arizona

For Leah Alder and Barbara O'Bagy

Editorial assistance by Margaret DeWitt Rooker, Cottonwood, California,
and Stacey Lynn, Tucson, Arizona.
Book design by Sanpete Publications.
Artwork and Layout by Terry Byron.
Typesetting by TYPES, Tucson, Arizona.
Printed by Arizona Lithographers, Tucson, Arizona.
Color Separations by Tru Colour, Inc., Phoenix, Arizona.

First printing 1990.
Second printing 1991.

Library of Congress Catalog card number 90-62945.
ISBN: 0-918080-75-4

Sanpete Publications
2751 West Monte Vista
Tucson, Arizona 85745

Foreword

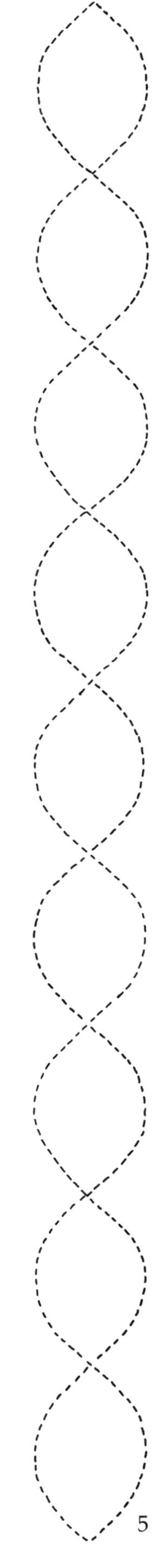

One cannot help but be impressed by the remarkable life of Dorinda Moody Slade. She experienced and endured so much: several moves, always to increasingly remote and raw frontiers; personal sacrifices for her chosen faith; and the heartbreaking losses of husbands and children. We know she endured these things from the facts and records left behind, and yet there is evidence of something beyond this. The legacy of handwork left by Dorinda Moody Slade reveals a triumph of spirit over the events and circumstances of her life. Although she left no written record in her own hand – no diary or journal – her quilts can tell us some of her story.

These quilts are material records of the qualities and talents of Dorinda Slade. We can see that she was imaginative, had a sure sense of color, and was patient and thorough, enough to cover her quilts with thousands of quilting stitches. But the very fact that the quilts exist, that she chose to create rather than dwell on her sorrows and losses, tells us even more.

The quilts are exceptional because of outstanding design and workmanship. The designs, mostly original interpretations of traditional patterns, show a unique sense of style and balance. Hard-edged, pieced patterns are framed by appliquéd borders, with sinuous vines and exuberant flowers. Appliquéd Rose of Sharon quilts are edged with geometric shapes, complementing the flowers within. Even simple patchwork patterns are sized and set in an impressive manner.

All the quilts, whether simple patterns or masterpieces such as the Sunburst, are quilted with designs that transcend the limitations of the quilt itself. The designs were obviously custom drawn for each quilt; the tiny cables, graceful feathers, and flowing curves exactly fit the various background shapes. In every case the quilting both complements the pattern of the quilt and adds further embellishment and beauty.

Although the quilts made by Dorinda Moody Slade are not technically perfect (many antique quilts show finer, tinier stitches), they are well made, which is important considering the difficulty of some of the patterns she chose. She favored designs that would showcase her skills. The narrow, pointed triangles, curved seams, and tiny appliquéd circles all indicate a maker who was confident in her abilities and perhaps a little proud of her expertise with the needle. As impressive as these quilts are, true appreciation of Dorinda Slade's abilities will come from attempting some of the actual patterns, drafted and presented in this volume.

When Carolyn Davis first saw a small black-and-white photograph of a quilt, and read the few lines about its maker, she couldn't have imagined where her curiosity would lead her. Years of research, extensive correspondence, and travel have culminated in this work. This volume is more than a mere biography of Dorinda Moody Slade; it is a history, telling of an unparalleled episode in the settling of the West; it is a mystery, which leaves unanswered questions about the lost quilts; it is a love story, where even death cannot end the love between husband and wife; and most of all, it is a tribute to an extraordinary woman.

Helen Young Frost

Contents

Preface

I first heard of Dorinda Moody Slade in 1984 when an aunt, knowing of my interest in quilting, sent a catalog of the quilt collection of the Daughters of Utah Pioneers Museum in Salt Lake City, Utah. In *Pioneer Quilts* there was a small, black-and-white photograph of Dorinda's 1866 Sunrise in the Pines quilt and a short biography of her life. Mild curiosity led to a long-distance telephone call to the museum to inquire if there was any further information available about Dorinda and her quilts. That first telephone call led to the Moody family and Dorinda's many descendants. Although among her daughters, her stepchildren, and her brothers' families there were no living descendants who knew and remembered Dorinda, there were generous numbers of her descendants in large Latter-day Saint (Mormon) families who knew and valued the stories of their pioneer ancestors.

Over the years my casual interest became nearly a full-time pursuit as the number of letters, telephone calls, and contacts with the Moody family, museums, and archives grew into the hundreds. In the search to pull together the century-old and far-flung stories of Dorinda's life, I discovered not only more of her quilts, but also many delightful members of her family who obviously shared her twinkling sense of humor, quick intelligence, and spontaneous warmth.

As time went by, a growing and compelling feeling, a feeling that time was running out, urged me to quickly get on with the research. Scattered across half a dozen western states was a generation of Dorinda's great-granddaughters, many of whom owned her treasured quilts, which they had inherited along with their mother's memories and stories of Dorinda's life. Through them I came to know Dorinda and to feel the tremendous pride they had in the endurance, courage, and, above all, the artistic genius exhibited in the life of their pioneer grandmother. Most of them in their eighties and nineties, they were now becoming frail in health, entering nursing homes, and slipping away.

Without exception, these wonderful ladies gave me encouragement and information, sharing my enthusiasm in the research project. Their frequent letters were always a boost and an incentive to continue searching for the missing parts of Dorinda's story. There was always an underlying feeling on my part that even though I couldn't personally know Dorinda, the friendships created through her with her great-granddaughters was a special gift to be enjoyed and treasured.

Special and yet typical of the associations I have enjoyed with Dorinda's great-granddaughters is the long-distance friendship that developed with Annie McMurtrey, a granddaughter of Dorinda's sixth daughter, Fredonia Forsyth. When I visited Annie in her Shelley, Idaho, home in 1987 she greeted my family with ice cream and homemade apple pie. Over the years she corresponded regularly, always interested in new information or quilts that I had located. When I wrote in 1989 that I had been invited to give a lecture on Dorinda at the International Quilt Festival in Houston, Texas, Annie replied that she wanted to help with the trip, and in the letter was a ten-dollar bill, a not inconsequential amount to this dear lady living on a tiny pension. Annie passed away on November 5, a day after the lecture and just two weeks short of her eighty-seventh birthday.

As the months of research turned into years, Dorinda came to occupy ever greater spaces of my life, and each new bit of information added to my growing respect and admiration for this simple, pioneer woman. Devotion to her religion compelled Dorinda to forsake her comfortable home in Texas and travel 1,500 miles by covered wagon to Salt Lake City, Utah. In order to travel with the wagon train, she entered into a marriage of convenience with a recent widower with eight children, while at the time she had five children of her own. This was not a commitment entered into lightly, as it spanned two decades of marriage and an even longer time as stepmother and grandmother. Clearly, Dorinda was a woman of strong moral and religious principles.

Dorinda's quilts threaded a constant theme throughout the different stages of her life. Her artistic impulses would not be held down under the burden of her daily workload. Sent by her church to settle in a remote mountain valley, Dorinda may have ultimately found the isolation a blessing – narrowing the scope of her physical world seemed to more sharply focus her creativity. Pine Valley is definitely remote. Its location is listed in ghost-town guidebooks, and, for the few remaining residents, electricity did not arrive in the valley until 1964. Before construction of a nearby ski resort, Pine Valley held the distinction of being the town with the highest elevation in Utah. Summers in the valley are delightful, but winters are defined by heavy snows that cut off travel and communication to the world outside the mountains.

In this lovely but faraway place, Dorinda spent the last four decades of her life serving her church and her family, and eventually there came to be time for her to devote to herself and her first love, quiltmaking. Through the years of research I came to know Dorinda Moody Slade as a woman of integrity and strength and, ultimately, as an artist. My life has been stretched and enriched through the association. I wouldn't have missed it for anything.

Carolyn Davis, September 1990

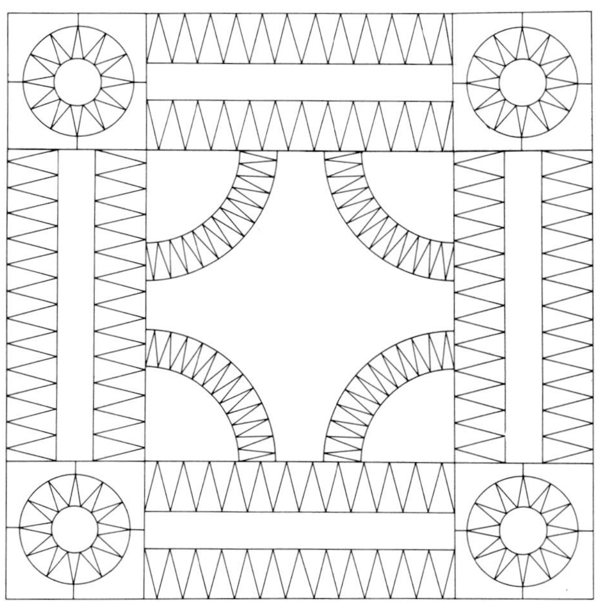

Sunrise in the Pines quilt block.

Dorinda Melissa Moody

Born Jan. 15, 1808. Iredell Co., NC
Died Nov. 21, 1895. Pine Valley, UT
Parents John Wyatt Moody and Mary "Polly" Baldwin

Spouse (1) William Gidson Salmon
Born Montgomery Co., AL
Died Dec. 3, 1834. Montgomery Co., AL
Married July 24, 1825.
Montgomery Co., AL

Children
1. Philina Angelina Salmon
   Born Dec. 8, 1826.
   Montgomery Co., AL
   Died Sept. 28, 1847. Harris Co., TX
   Married William Brooks, Jan. 27, 1847
2. Margaret Frances Salmon
   Born Sept. 7, 1829.
   Montgomery Co., AL
   Died Oct. 10, 1831.
   Montgomery Co., AL
3. Marginia Levenia Salmon
   Born Sept. 2, 1833.
   Montgomery Co., AL
   Died Jan. 3, 1846. Harris Co., TX

Spouse (2) Michael Roup Goheen
Born Dec. 23, 1807. Chattliwassa,
Columbia Co., PA
Died June 16, 1850. Spring Creek, TX
Parents Edward Goheen &
Christina Roup
Married Apr. 25, 1837. Bastrop,
Fayette Co., TX
Sealed Mar. 8, 1884

Children
1. Eliza Adeline Goheen
   Born July 21, 1838. Bastrop, TX
   Died Dec. 29, 1922. Pine Valley, UT
   Married Robert Lewis Lloyd,
   Jan. 8, 1852
2. Christiana (Christa) Elizabeth Goheen
   Born Sept. 9, 1841. Harris Co., TX
   Died Aug. 24, 1892. Panguitch, UT
   Married Seguine Cooper, Mar. 3, 1857
3. Fredonia Melissa Goheen
   Born Sept. 10, 1845. Spring Creek, TX
   Died Oct. 18, 1917, Salt Lake City, UT
   Married Thomas Robert Forsyth,
   Apr. 15, 1863
4. Louisa Jane Goheen
   Born Dec. 23, 1847. Harris Co., TX
   Died July 17, 1908. Eager, Arizona
   Married Benjamin Brown,
   Oct. 29, 1864
5. Michael Goheen
   Born Feb. 2, 1850. Harris Co., TX
   Died July 8, 1853. Cherokee Nation

Spouse (3) William Rufous Slade (Washington Slocum)
Born July 1, 1811. Rensselaer Co., NY
Died Nov. 28, 1872. Panaca, Lincoln Co., NV
Parents John Slocum & Phebe Slade
Married (1) Julia Ann Higgenbotham,
Oct. 24, 1832
Died Nov. 28, 1852. Harris Co., TX

Married (2) Dorinda Melissa Moody Goheen,
Feb. 20, 1853

Children from first marriage
to Julia Ann Higgenbotham
1. William Slade
   Born Feb. 18, 1834. Oplanca, LA
   Died Oct. 4, 1902. Colonial Dublan,
   Chihuahua, Mex.
2. Martha Slade
   Born Oct. 10, 1835. Oplanca, LA
   Died Oct. 14, 1835. Oplanca, LA
3. Jefferson Slade
   Born Sept. 22, 1836. Oplanca, LA
   Died Dec. 24, 1915
4. Mary Jane Margiana Slade
   Born Apr. 22, 1838. Oplanca, LA
   Died July 26, 1840. Jefferson, TX
5. Albert Slade
   Born Dec. 20, 1839. Jefferson, TX
   Died July 19, 1853. Cherokee Nation
6. Clara Elizabeth Slade
   Born Dec. 25, 1842. Jefferson, TX
   Died Aug. 25, 1891
7. Benjamin Slade
   Born Apr. 22, 1843. Harris Co., TX
   Died Aug., 1847. Harris Co., TX
8. John Slade
   Born July 21, 1845. Harris Co., TX
   Died July 18, 1853. Cherokee Nation
9. Henry Slade
   Born Nov. 26, 1847. Harris Co., TX
   Died Jan. 6, 1934
10. Alice Slade
    Born Sept. 12, 1849. Harris Co., TX
    Died Aug. 16, 1853. Cherokee Nation
11. James McGow Slade
    Born Apr. 29, 1851. Harris Co., TX
    Died June 17, 1871

Slade genealogy courtesy of Vonna Polad.

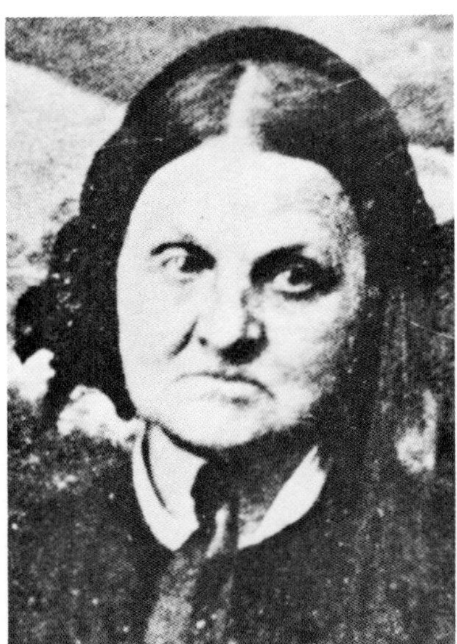

Dorinda Slade.

Pine Tree Quilt, c. 1880.

The Pine Tree quilt top was hand pieced by Dorinda from fabric she had dyed. Mountain mahogany was used for the brown tree trunks, and indigo grown in the Washington area was used for blue, which was then overdyed with yellow obtained from cedar berries to create green. Over the years the yellow has faded away, leaving only blue in the Pine Tree blocks. The quilt top, carried in Louisa Brown's wagon during the 1880 journey over the Honeymoon Trail, was quilted years later by the women of the Brown family in their Arizona home. The deceptively plain appearing Pine Tree quilt contains almost 1,500 pieces. Each of the twenty Pine Tree blocks consists of sixty-six triangles and squares stitched together by hand.

Quilt courtesy of Marjorie Merrill Ransom. Photo by Daniel Henry Seaman, Eager, Arizona.

Detail of Pine Tree quilt.

In the early months of 1853, forty-five-year-old Dorinda Moody Goheen was in the midst of selling her property and preparing to join a wagon train of Mormon converts leaving for Salt Lake City, Utah. It had been two years since Dorinda had joined the Church of Jesus Christ of Latter-day Saints just a month after the death of her second husband, Michael Roup Goheen. Dorinda was a woman well acquainted with sorrow. Her first marriage in 1824 to William Gidson Salmon had ended after only seven years when William died as a result of drinking poisoned whiskey. Dorinda grieved over William's death, but this second tragedy, the loss of Michael, who had been a tender and loving husband during the thirteen years of their marriage, nearly threw her into despair. This was the passion she never forgot. In her heart Michael was always the true love of her life. The year Michael died, 1850, Dorinda was forty-two years old and the mother of five children who ranged in age from five months to twelve years. Almost immediately after Michael's death, she began making preparations to leave Texas and travel to Utah, to live in the chosen land of her new church.

In the years before his marriage, Michael had served in the Texas army and achieved the rank of captain. As recompense for his years of service, he had received large grants of land from the Texas government. Dorinda and Michael developed this property into a thriving cotton farm with an adjacent dairy, enterprises that now had to be disposed of. Nonetheless, Dorinda resolved to take with her to Utah most of the herd of cattle that

Dorinda's hand-sewn dresses with the long, full sleeves gathered and buttoned at the wrists were often topped with one of her handmade, white, lace collars. Her long, full skirts had as many as four widths of fabric. Although Dorinda was a tiny woman, there was a proud and erect set to her shoulders. In this photograph, her graceful hands, with their long, straight fingers, are still strong and capable. Only in her face is there a reflection of the years of care and toil she has seen.

the Goheens ran north of their farm in Spring Creek Canyon. Preparations for leaving included making provisions for the many slaves who had worked for years in Dorinda's home and in the Goheen cotton fields. In a move that surely went against local thought and decades of her own practice, Dorinda freed them all.

Dorinda selected the few belongings and necessities that would furnish a new home on an unsettled frontier. Along with her quilts, an unfinished cross-stitch sampler and her treasured handwoven cotton coverlet, Dorinda packed into the wagon her baking oven and the large, cast-iron cooking kettle. By early February 1853, Dorinda was nearly ready to join the Preston Thomas wagon train of emigrants bound for Utah. She would make the 1,500-mile journey in a wagon built by her beloved late husband, Michael Goheen.

As travel preparations neared completion it became apparent that the long, dangerous journey ahead – with children to care for, teams to drive, and cattle and oxen to herd – would be more than a woman alone could manage. In the emigrant group was another family with a similar problem. William Slade's wife of twenty years had died two months earlier, leaving William alone to care for eight children aged two to nineteen. Like Dorinda, William faced sorrow and loss in addition to the exhausting work involved in an overland journey by wagon. Only days before the wagon train left, Dorinda and William were married on February 20, 1853. Their marriage was one of convenience, a working arrangement that enabled both of them to pursue the dream of many Mormon converts to live in Utah, the land of their new religion. Together with their combined family of thirteen children, Dorinda and William set out in the spring of 1853 to "gather to Zion."

Gone to Texas

Dorinda Melissa Moody was born on January 15, 1808, in Iredell County, North Carolina. She was the first child of Mary "Polly" Baldwin and John Wyatt Moody. Her father, John, was the oldest of the eleven children of Dr. Thomas and Mary Young Moody. Born on June 10, 1776, in Lunenburg County, West Virginia, John moved at the age of thirteen with his family to Surrey County, West Virginia. In 1806 he married twenty-one-year-old Mary Polly Baldwin. Polly, born on February 1, 1775, in Wilkes County, Georgia, was the daughter of Francis Baldwin and Rhoda Jennings. Dorinda was close to eight years old by the time her brothers came along. Polly lost the next two babies, but three sons survived: Francis Winfred, born in 1816; William Cresfield, born in 1819; and last, John Monroe, born in 1822 when Dorinda was fourteen.

The family moved to St. Clair County, Alabama, when Dorinda was a small child. They remained there about ten years until 1819 when they moved to Covey County, Alabama. Unfortunately, the climate there proved too hot for John Moody's health, so the family returned to St. Clair County. Later the Moodys lived in Montgomery County, Alabama, and for a short time in Creek Indian Territory.

The motive for these frequent moves was an urge commonly called "westering," an urge inspired at this time by the exploration and opening of new lands for settlement. A family could often acquire a homestead merely for the price of the labor to clear the land for planting and building. As Dorinda's parents moved from one piece of land to the next, they cleared the fields and planted crops. Cotton was the major crop raised by the Moody family in Alabama and later in Texas. (Decades afterward on the Utah frontier, cotton again played a primary role in Dorinda's life when she was called to be a pioneer colonizer of the Cotton Mission in southwestern Utah. It was cotton that shaped her skills until her art shaped the cotton.)

As a young girl, Dorinda displayed a superior skill in needlecrafts. Due to a shortage of labor, Polly Moody helped in the fields while her young daughter followed the pattern that would frame the days of much of her future life. Dorinda assumed responsibility for care of the younger children along with the duties of domestic work, including, perhaps most important in terms of her later art, spinning and weaving the cotton raised on the family farm. During this time Dorinda perfected her needlecraft skills, and her love for creating with thread and fabric blossomed. The weaving and quilting could be intertwined with the demands of child care. Furthermore, needlework, an acceptable, even a required, skill for nineteenth-century women, was often the only creative path possible given the frequency and immediacy of tasks related to raising children. A woman could pick up a piece of cloth, stitch a moment, lay it aside to stir a pot or soothe a cry, and return to the piece again. For Dorinda, quiltmaking evolved from a pragmatic skill, practiced against a background demanding daily labor, into a uniquely inspired artistic format that combined her needle skills with her sense of color and design to create lasting images of beauty on a fabric canvas.

One of Dorinda's earliest known creations was made while she was in her teens. According to a description written by Ella Caroline Lloyd, a granddaughter, it was a homespun, handwoven quilt the natural color of

Dorinda's cross-stitched and embroidered sampler was completed when she was eighteen years old and living in Alabama. The sampler is signed:

Dorinda • Meliꝫꝫa • Moody • her ꝫamPler • 1826.

Sampler courtesy of Cleo Greenwood.

the cotton, covered with hand-stitched designs. A large basket of flowers, feathers, and ferns was worked in the center, and smaller baskets of flowers and ferns were stitched in each corner. Twenty-eight different decorative stitches were used, and, around the edges of the spread, Dorinda netted a six-inch-wide fringe.

The description of this coverlet indicates that it may have been a whole-cloth or whitework quilt. Whole-cloth quilts were very popular in the early 1800s at about the time Dorinda would have made this one, but the style gradually declined in use and virtually disappeared by the end of the Civil War according to Barbara Brackman in *Clues in the Calico*. Constructed of large pieces of fabric seamed together for the top, a filler, and a lining, such a quilt was generally white or, as indicated in this instance, "the natural color of cotton." Whole-cloth quilts had no color, piecing, or appliqué work added. Designs were created through close, meticulous stitching, sometimes with the addition of cording, stuffing, and fringes. Stitching was done with white thread on white fabric, generally with a central medallion motif. Because of the impressive amount and variety of stitches, whitework quilts were often made to showcase a needlewoman's proficiency. In *Quilts in America*, Patsy and Myron Orlofsky note that it was not uncommon for a whole-cloth quilt to contain more than a million stitches. This early coverlet of Dorinda's, which she carried with her on all subsequent moves, stayed in her possession for the rest of her life. Later it was passed on to a granddaughter, but, unfortunately, it has been lost.

At seventeen, while her family was residing in Montgomery County, Alabama, Dorinda met William Gidson Salmon. His history and family background remain as yet undiscovered. The couple was married on July 24, 1825, and a year and a half later, the first of their three daughters, Philina Angelina, was born.

As a young wife confined to home while awaiting the birth of her first child, Dorinda worked on a meticulously sewn cross-stitch linen sampler. Possibly it was an exercise to practice her letters, a common task for young women of her time, as the sampler features five different styles of the alphabet and two of numbering. Her alphabets use the older, eighteenth-century style of writing the **Q** as the reverse of **P**. (The modern form of **Q** did not come into common usage until later in the nineteenth century.[1]) Her name is stitched on the bottom line as **Dorinda Melissa Moody** and the year given is 1826. The simplest explanation for the use of her maiden name is that she had begun the sampler before her marriage. At age eighteen, Dorinda was much older than the young schoolgirls who typically worked a sampler. In the early 1800s it was more common for eight- to twelve-year-old girls to make samplers for practicing their letters and stitches. However, in later years Dorinda rarely spoke of William Salmon, and the use of her maiden name on the sampler, along with other hints, may have implied unhappiness with her marriage. Although never completed (one tree was left unstitched), the cross-stitch sampler is the only piece of Dorinda's needlework from her early days in Alabama to have survived into the twentieth century.

Obviously, to have been carefully stored away, protected from dirt and water, and carried with her on two arduous overland journeys by wagon many years afterward, the sampler had greater importance to

Dorinda's bonnet.
Courtesy of Annie McMurtrey.

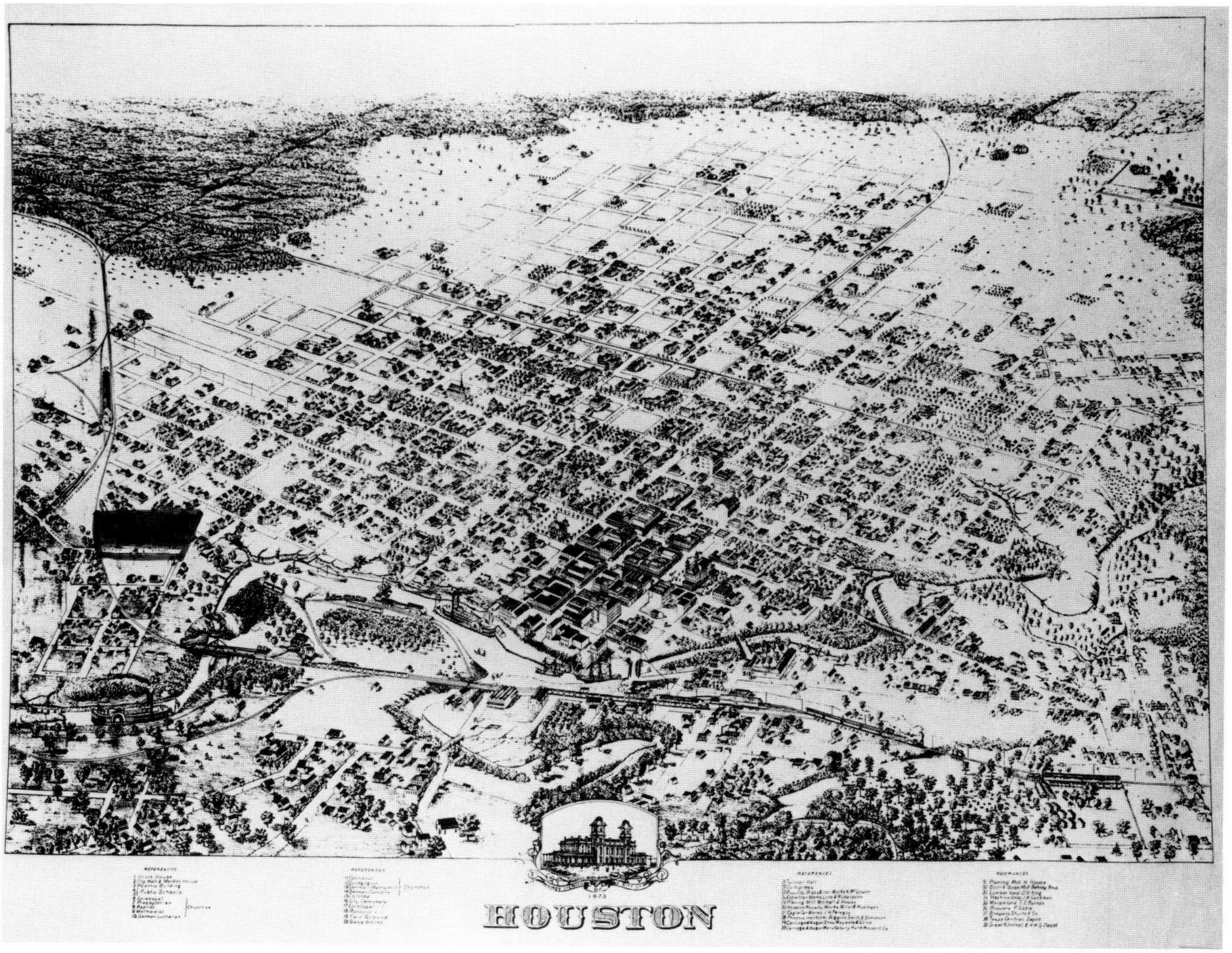

The darkened area to the left on this early Houston map shows the location of the John and Polly Moody farm located in what is now the downtown business district of the city of Houston, Texas. "Moody Street" runs along the northern boundary of John's and Polly's farm.

1873 Bird's Eye View of Houston by A. Koch. Photo courtesy of Houston Public Library.

Check made out to himself by John Wyatt Moody and signed over to V[alentine] Bennett for the amount he had borrowed from Bennett to pay rent. John Moody was the first auditor of the Republic of Texas, a position he held until his death in 1839. His distinctive signature was discovered in the Texas archives by Moody family historians searching for genealogical documents. Once the signature was identified, archivists were able to document the numerous papers John Moody had signed in his years as auditor.

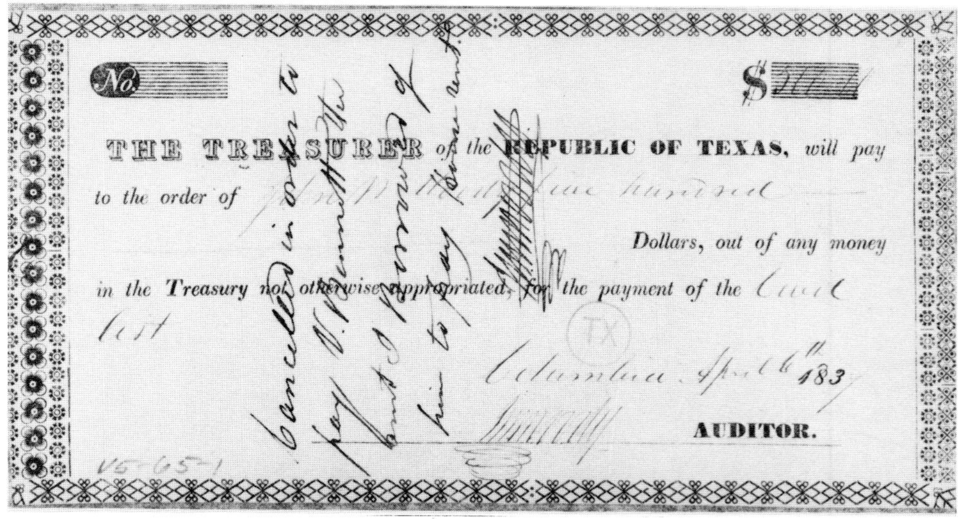

No. $

THE TREASURER of the REPUBLIC OF TEXAS, will pay to the order of

Dollars, out of any money in the Treasury not otherwise appropriated, for the payment of the

AUDITOR.

John Wyatt Moody Check, Comptroller of Public Accounts Records (RG304), Archives Division, Texas State Library.

I certify that M. R. Gohen has faithfully served and discharged the duties of captain in the army of Texas under my command since the 24 of September last. By his zeal, patriotism and fidelity he has contributed much to the public service and I recommend him to the attention of my successor as he has this day resigned his commission as captain his company have been nearly dissolved by the number who have returned home

Head Quarters before Bexar Nov. 24. 1835.

S. F. Austin
Com. in Chief

San Felipe De Austin
before me John W Moody Auditor Come M. R. Goheen and says the above Instrument is Just and true and original Sworn to 20th Jany 1836
before J W Moody Auditor

Letter discharging Michael Roup Goheen from his duties as captain in the Army of Texas, signed by Stephen F. Austin, Commander-in-Chief. The additional note authorizing Michael's pay is signed by John Wyatt Moody, auditor of the Republic of Texas and Michael's future father-in-law.

Stephen F. Austin letter on behalf of M. R. Goheen, Comptroller of Public Accounts Records (RG304), Archives Division, Texas State Library.

Dorinda than a mere learning exercise in stitchery. Today, a century and a half after its creation, the sampler is a treasured heirloom.

Dorinda's and William's family continued to grow with the arrival of a second daughter, Margaret Frances, on September 7, 1829. Four years later, on September 2, 1833, a third daughter, Marginia Levenia, was born. There are many hints indicating unhappiness in the Salmon union, and the death of their two-year-old, Margaret, from membranous croup must have been a terrible blow to the marriage. William was away from home much of the time, and it was on a business trip in 1834 that he died after drinking poisoned whiskey. It is unknown whether William's death was accidental or a deliberate poisoning. That whiskey was recorded as the cause of his death may be another clue that the Salmon marriage was an unhappy one for Dorinda.

Snowball Quilt.
The Snowball quilt was hand pieced by Dorinda and quilted decades later by her great-granddaughter Rayola Gibson in Franklin, Idaho.
Quilt courtesy of Rayola Gibson.

Left a widow at the age of twenty-six, Dorinda had to find a means of supporting her daughters, aged seven and one. For a while she worked as a domestic helper, and eventually she was able to support her daughters by selling her quilts, laces, woven spreads, and other needlework, not an uncommon livelihood for a woman at that time, but a hard and meager one. That she could support her family by this method attests to Dorinda's skills. Since it usually took hours of work to produce pennies of compensation, she must have worked swiftly, and since there were many needleworkers, her skills must have been superior.

A year passed, and then, the extended Moody family, with the exception of the oldest son, moved to Texas, lured by the promise of free land and the hope that a different climate would be beneficial to Mr. Moody's failing health.[2] "Gone to Texas" was the popular phrase that described the migration of thousands of people such as the Moody family who traveled to Texas during the 1830s, drawn by visions of adventure or prosperity in the sparsely settled new land. Arriving in Texas in the fall of 1835, the younger sons, John and William, promptly joined the Army of the Republic of Texas, but since independence was won from Mexico in March 1836, they never fought a battle. However, as a result of their service, both brothers received large land grants. Each was given a Spanish league, approximately 4,409 acres, located in Anderson, Texas.[3]

John and Polly Moody settled on a farm on the outskirts of Houston, then capital of the Republic of Texas. The land in Harris County that

Detail of Snowball quilt.

comprised the Moody farm is now a part of the business section of downtown Houston. John Moody became auditor of public accounts in 1835 and held that position until his death of congestive fever four years later.

Dorinda moved into a small home near her parents and continued to support her daughters through the sale of her stitchery and other domestic sewing work. The year following her move to Texas she met a handsome young soldier, Michael Roup Goheen, a captain with the Army of the Republic of Texas. It is probable that one of her brothers knew Michael through the service and brought the eligible gentleman to meet their young widowed sister.

Michael, the son of Edward and Christiana Goheen, was born in Columbia County, Pennsylvania, on December 23, 1807. The Goheen family later moved to Genessea, Livingston County, New York, where Michael was educated in a military school.

Dorinda and Michael were married on April 25, 1837, in Bastrop, Texas. At twenty-nine and with two children, Dorinda had at last found the love of her life. Although the times to come were not without some hardship and heartache, her thirteen years with Michael were always recalled as the best of her life. Soon after their marriage, Michael also received a large land grant for his service with the army, and the family moved to Anderson, Texas.

These were busy, joyful years for the Goheens, raising a family and building a home. Because of the "Texas Northers," severe winds that swept down across the plains, Michael built a large, single-storied, low house with a dugout nearby that offered protection from the winds. Trained as a blacksmith and wheelwright, Michael made farm implements and wagons to sell. The Goheens owned slaves, and with their labor they raised cotton. They also had dairy cows, and in Spring Creek Canyon they ran a large herd of beef cattle.

Eliza

Eliza Adeline was the first of four daughters born to Michael and Dorinda Goheen on their Texas farm. Eliza inherited her mother's endurance and ability to cope with rugged frontier life, as she grew up riding horses and helping with the heavy work of cattle ranching and cotton farming. At the age of thirteen she married thirty-year-old Robert Lewis Lloyd, a ranch hand who had come to work for the Goheens as a young boy sixteen years earlier.

Eliza's and Robert's first child was born the following year in an abandoned army fort as the family traveled over the Old Spanish Trail from Texas to Utah. The Lloyds settled in Washington, Utah, where the covered wagon box served as a home during their first year in Dixie. After a willow and adobe shelter was constructed, the wagon box was used for years as Eliza's dairy house.

The Lloyds raised cotton in Washington, and Eliza was exceptionally skilled at spinning and weaving their homegrown cotton into fine, evenly textured fabric. Eliza spent many summer months at her mother's home to escape the heat of the low desert country, and she and Robert eventually moved to Pine Valley, where the last of their twelve children were born. Robert served Pine Valley for twenty years as justice of the peace and also used his rudimentary medical skills for setting bones and drawing teeth. After Robert's death in 1892, Eliza lived alone for the next thirty years in the brick house Robert had built for her.

Photo courtesy of Berenice Chadburn Liebhardt.

Christiana

In the spring of 1857, the year in which Dorinda moved to southern Utah, her fifth daughter, sixteen-year-old Christiana, married Seguine Cooper. The young man was a son of family friends from Spring Creek, Texas. The Coopers had converted to the Mormon faith and traveled to Utah at about the same time as Dorinda's family. Christiana and Seguine remained in northern Utah, residing in Fort Harriman, just south of Salt Lake City, while Christiana's mother and her family traveled on to southern Utah.

Eight years after their marriage, the Coopers were called by the church to settle in Dixie, near the Muddy River. They were instructed to take enough food, seed, and provisions to survive for one year. Because drought and heat made the living conditions so difficult, the family moved again and spent the next six years in Panaca, Nevada. Christiana was only eighty miles from Pine Valley, so she was able to make occasional visits to her mother and sisters.

In 1871, the Coopers moved a last time to a ranch near Panguitch in south-central Utah. Here the last three of Christiana's and Seguine's ten children were born.

Photo from *The John Wyatt Moody Family: Past and Present*. Permission to reproduce photo granted by E. Grant Moody.

Their first daughter, Eliza Adeline, was born on July 21, 1838, a year after their marriage. Shortly after Eliza's birth an episode occurred that caused Dorinda terrible remorse throughout her life. When Philina (Dorinda's oldest daughter by William Salmon), or Angelina, as she was generally called, was about fourteen she fell wildly in love with a ranch hand named Ruben. When Dorinda discovered this romance, she sent Ruben away and sent Angelina to attend school in Houston. However, when she learned that Ruben was still calling on Angelina, she brought her daughter back, ordering her never to see Ruben again. As the months passed, Angelina never recovered from her lost love. She cried for hours at a time and prayed for death by which she hoped eventually to be reunited with her lover. Dorinda, belatedly realizing her mistake and recognizing the likelihood that Angelina would never forget Ruben, searched for him and advertised for him in the papers, but Ruben never returned.

Meanwhile, in 1841 a second daughter, Christiana Elizabeth, was born to Michael and Dorinda, and Fredonia Melissa followed four years later. This brought the number of their children to four daughters, including Dorinda's two children from her first marriage. These years certainly held great happiness, but heartache came in the next year. The first blow struck when thirteen-year-old Marginia died. Shortly after the death of her sister, nineteen-year-old Angelina, who never really stopped loving her Ruben, reluctantly married William Brooks, a neighbor. The second tragedy followed within the year, when Angelina and her twin babies died just hours after the births on September 28, 1847. Mother and babies were buried in the same grave. Dorinda believed that Angelina had died of a broken heart and forever held herself responsible for Angelina's death. These events left Dorinda with no children from her marriage to William Salmon, and once again she was expecting a child.[4]

Three months after Angelina's death, Dorinda's and Michael's fourth daughter, Louisa Jane, was born on her father's fortieth birthday, December 23, 1847. The Goheen family now included four daughters, and for Dorinda it must have been a busy and a sad time at once. Because Michael was required to spend time away on business trips and to manage their cattle herd in Spring Creek, Dorinda was often left alone to oversee and care for (with the help of slaves) their house, the dairy farm, and the cotton crop. While Dorinda was not physically responsible for all the domestic work of the Goheen farm, she had to exert great organizational energy to keep the work running smoothly and to feed and clothe not only her family, but also the many servants and field workers living on the farm. Given Dorinda's love of quilting, it is likely that she continued to piece and quilt whenever she could find a free moment. However, none of the quilts that she made during these years have survived into the twentieth century.

Another of Dorinda's responsibilities, and one she apparently took quite seriously, was her children's education. The extent of her own formal education is unknown. Certainly, as auditor of public accounts, her father, John Moody, would have been an intelligent and educated man. For Dorinda, however, the opportunity for extended schooling probably was precluded owing to the numerous family moves to increasingly remote frontier areas during her childhood. The need for Dorinda to help in the cotton fields, and in the home with spinning, weaving, and child care, along with her marriage to William Salmon at age seventeen, point to the likelihood that whatever schooling she received was spotty and consisted only of informal lessons at home.

Sunrise in the Pines Quilt, 101½″ x 85½″, c. 1866.
The Sunrise in the Pines quilt was a wedding gift from Dorinda to her younger brother, William, on the occasion of his marriage to his fourth wife, Louisa Williams. This magnificent quilt is made of hand-dyed cotton fabric and is entirely hand pieced with more than 3,400 pieces.

Quilt courtesy of Daughters of Utah Pioneers Museum, Salt Lake City, Utah. Photo by Busath Photography, Salt Lake City, Utah.

Sunrise in the Pines quilt detail.

Quilt courtesy of Daughters of Utah Pioneers Museum, Salt Lake City, Utah. Photo by Busath Photography, Salt Lake City, Utah.

Brief as Dorinda's formal education may have been, descendants recalled that in Texas when her children were young, Dorinda taught "spelling, arithmetic, a little geography, and history" in her home to her daughters and to the neighborhood children. As her daughters reached the age of nine or ten, Dorinda made arrangements for them to board with families in town in order to attend school. In this Dorinda exhibited a high respect for education, unusual at that time, particularly regarding the education of girls. Angelina had apparently inherited her mother's talent for art and music, and Dorinda provided her with opportunities to attend a young women's school in Houston for several months of the year during her teenage years. Similarly, from the time Eliza was nine years old she spent at least five months in town each winter boarding with a family or with her Grandmother Moody in Houston in order to attend school.

In 1850 a fifth child was born to Michael and Dorinda. Their only son, named for his father, was born on the second of February. Later that spring missionaries came to the area to preach the teachings of Joseph Smith and the young Mormon church, established only twenty years earlier, to the people in Harris County. Dorinda and Michael were Methodists, but hearing the Mormon message, they decided to be baptized in the Church of Jesus Christ of Latter-day Saints. Since it was then early summer, Michael first had to return to his cattle ranch to supervise a livestock sale. Dorinda never saw him again. While in Spring Creek, he grew suddenly ill with a congestive chill and died on June 16, 1850. Michael was just forty-three years old. He was buried in Spring Creek before Dorinda even received the news of his death. Once again Dorinda was a widow, this time with four daughters and an infant son. Six weeks after Michael's death, on July 28, Dorinda was baptized in the Mormon church by Elders Preston Thomas and James McGow.

Michael's death was a devastating blow to Dorinda. He had been a kind and loving husband, and in later years she always referred to him as "the love of my life." Clearly, Michael's death cast a deep loss in her life.

Nineteen-year-old Jacob Peart, Jr., carved this cotton plant into the black cliff near the Peart farm at Heberville on the confluence of Santa Clara Creek and the Virgin River. The inscription reads, "I was se[n]t her[e] to rais[e] cotten March 1858 JACOB PEART."
From the Lynne Clark Collection, St. George, Utah.

Her newly chosen religion was a great consolation, however, and soon her extended family chose to convert to the Mormon faith. Dorinda's mother, Polly Moody, was baptized in the fall of 1850, and William Moody, Dorinda's younger brother, converted the following year.

Perhaps because of the influence of "westering" in their formative years, but also because of the urge to "gather to Zion," William, Dorinda, and their mother, Polly, decided to sell out their holdings in Texas and move to Utah, chosen land of the Mormons.

On January 8, 1852, Dorinda's oldest daughter, Eliza, married a Mormon convert, Robert Lewis Lloyd, who helped them with the travel preparations. Eliza was only thirteen years old and Robert was thirty, but this time Dorinda voiced no objections to a daughter's early marriage, and the wedding was held in her home. Although a great deal older than Eliza, Robert was no stranger to the family, having worked for them for sixteen years. Even though the couple's age difference was greater than the bride's lifetime, Robert had a lot to recommend him. Orphaned at three and taken in by an older sister, he learned early to take care of himself. He began working on Michael Goheen's Texas farm at thirteen, two years before Eliza was born. He had gained rudimentary medical training at an earlier job working for a doctor, and this proved a valuable asset in Texas and later on the Utah frontier. Furthermore, his steady, hardworking habits endeared him to the Goheens. Perhaps Dorinda even viewed him almost as a son, having seen him grow to manhood at her Texas home. And through the following decades of their lives in Utah, Robert and Eliza always lived near Dorinda and shared with her a close family relationship.

Dorinda's brother William decided to take his wife, Harriet, and five children over the more developed route to Utah, crossing the Gulf of Mexico, traveling up the Mississippi River, then riding overland in wagons from Keokuk, Iowa, to Salt Lake City. Traveling with William was his mother, Polly Moody, brother John's wife, Margaret, and her four children. John, planning to join them later in Utah, accompanied the family as far as Galveston, then returned home to attend to family business matters. But once back in Harris County, John discovered the hateful prejudice then raging against Mormons when he received threats against his life. Realizing

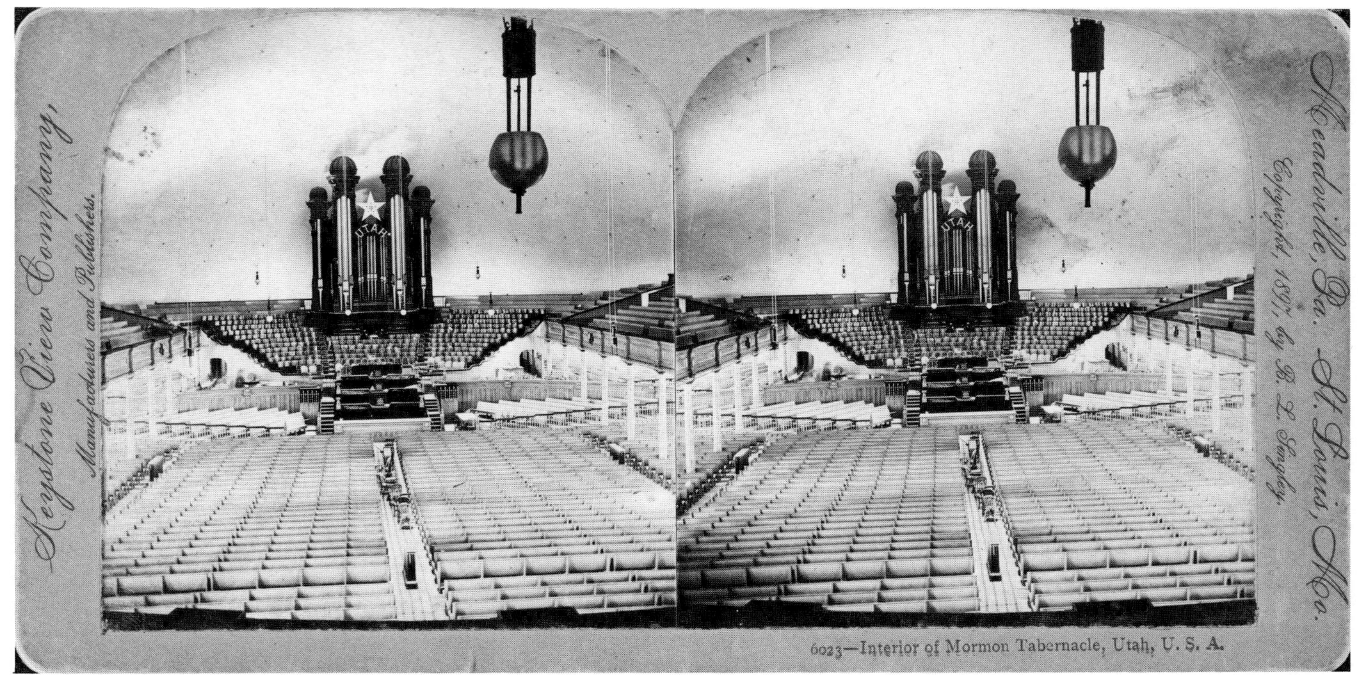

The world-famous organ in the Mormon Tabernacle in Salt Lake City was built from the yellow pines that grew in Left Hand Fork in Pine Valley Canyon. In *Under Dixie Sun* Bessie Snow relates that Robert Gardner, an early Pine Valley settler and lumberman, hand picked the yellow pines for Joseph Ridges' organ. The trees were felled, cut to suitable lengths, and loaded onto a freighting wagon. Robert's daughter Sarah and her fiance, William Meeks, hauled the wagonload of lumber on their wedding journey to Salt Lake City, where they were married in the Endowment House.

The stereoscopic view of the tabernacle shows the huge Ridges organ. The star on the organ commemorates Utah's statehood in 1896. Author's collection.

he was already considered a Mormon, he chose to be baptized in the church in the summer of 1853 and was reunited with his family in September 1854.

Dorinda had been close to her mother, especially after Michael's death, when Polly, having also experienced the loss of her husband, gave Dorinda much-needed emotional support. As the pain of Michael's loss eased, mother and daughter worked together, planning their move to Utah and the new lives they would build in the "promised valley." Sadly, Dorinda never saw her mother again. Polly Moody made the difficult overland journey to Salt Lake City, but she died on December 10, 1853, just a few weeks after her arrival in Utah.

Meanwhile, Dorinda had freed her slaves and sold her property, which was listed in the 1850 census as having a value of $400.00, a moderately prosperous sum on the Texas frontier at that time. She resolved to take a herd of her Texas longhorn cattle and some other livestock with her to Utah, a challenging undertaking for a single woman with young children. She had an ox team to pull her wagon, which was compactly loaded with more than a thousand pounds of required provisions.

Dorinda packed flour, cornmeal, sugar, and dried fruit for the journey. There were tools, clothes and bedding, seeds for her garden, flower seeds for her yard, and cuttings for fruit trees and rose bushes. Pots, churns, and water barrels were lashed to the sides of the wagon, along with a baking oven and a huge cast-iron kettle. Into her wooden trunk she carefully laid her quilts, including her treasured woven coverlet and the

Sunburst Quilt, 91″ x 81½″, c. 1880-1890.

Dorinda hand pieced the exquisite Sunburst quilt with tiny, colored calico prints on a white background. It was then heavily quilted in a graceful and original design. The heavy quilting may have helped to preserve the quilt, as Dorinda's granddaughter used it for many years in the hotel she ran in Panguitch, Utah. Today the Sunburst quilt is a treasured Kerr family heirloom.

Quilt courtesy of Colleen Haycock Kerr. Photo by Busath Photography, Salt Lake City, Utah.

Sunburst quilt detail.

cross-stitch sampler made decades earlier in Alabama, along with a supply of fabric that had been woven from cotton grown on her Harris County farm. Last, she packed her sewing box, spinning wheel, and quilting frames. Dorinda was now ready to join the other converts on a wagon train that was being organized under the direction of Preston Thomas, a Mormon missionary from Utah.

Another member of the wagon train was also faced with the difficulty of traveling alone with young children. William Rufous Slade was a cotton farmer from Louisiana who came to Texas hoping to acquire some of the free land. William was born Washington Slocum on July 1, 1811, in Pittstown, New York, the eighth child of John and Phebe Slocum. The Slocums were a prosperous family and their children were educated by private tutors rather than at the public schools. Family stories about the rift between William and his parents and reasons why he left home vary. One version is that William ran away to escape the confines of his schooling, another that he took money from his father, and still another that he was running from troubles with the law. At any rate, William assumed a new first name and his mother's maiden name, Slade, and left his parents' home forever when he was about sixteen. By the time he was twenty-one he had made his way to Louisiana, where he married Julia Ann Higgenbotham. Their first four children were born on their cotton farm in Oplanca.

In Texas, Julia Ann and William settled on a cotton farm neighboring the Goheen land in Harris County, where in the course of years they had seven more children. The 1850 census lists them as having adjoining farms and records the value of William Slade's property at $300.00. The Slades too were recent converts to the Mormon church and were also preparing to go to Utah. However, shortly before they were to leave, Julia Ann became very ill and died.

The wagon train of converts was in the midst of final preparations for leaving, and there seems to have been no time for turning back, so as a

William Rufous Slade, Dorinda's third husband, 1811-1872.

matter of mutual convenience, eleven weeks after Julia Ann's death, William and Dorinda were married on February 20, 1853. At age forty-five Dorinda now had a family that included her five children by Michael (whose ages ranged from three to fifteen), Robert (Eliza's husband), and now William Slade's eight children: William, age nineteen; Jefferson, age seventeen; Albert, age fourteen; Clara, age twelve; John, age eight; Henry, age six; Alice, age four; and James, age two. Together they were a family of sixteen. Another young member of the Slade group was Mose, a former slave and lifelong friend of William's oldest son. Mose went with the family to Utah, where he lived until his death in the 1870s.

Traveling in wagons that Michael Goheen had built, the Slades and Goheens left Texas in the spring of 1853, heading northwest through the dangerous and unsettled Indian territory. As they reached the Red River, the boundary between Texas and Oklahoma, illness struck the wagon train, and many of the converts died. It is not known exactly what disease hit the emigrant train, although family histories refer to it as either "black canker" or "Texas mountain fever." Among the victims was three-year-old Michael, Dorinda's only son, who died on July 8. Surely this loss following Michael's death must have been devastating. In addition, two of William's children, John and Albert, died – one on July 18 and the other on July 19. A month later, little Alice, William's four-year-old daughter, died. Six-year-old Louisa was also struck with the disease and was dangerously ill for a time, but fortunately she recovered.

Devastated by the sickness, leaders of the wagon train decided to take refuge in an abandoned army fort in Cherokee Nation. The Saints, as they were often referred to in the Mormon church, moved into the vacant homes, settling in to give themselves and their livestock a much-needed rest from travel, illness, and threatening Indians. There Dorinda unpacked and set up her quilting frames in an abandoned mill. She now had time for quilting since the usual burdens of seasonal work (putting in crops, harvesting, and storing food) and the domestic burdens such as making soap, candles, and all other necessities of a pioneer home were temporarily lifted. More important, the soothing repetition of the quilting was a comfort to Dorinda as she worked through the devastating loss of her only son, Michael, and the deaths of her three young stepchildren.

While at the fort, Dorinda completed a quilt for Melissa Meeks, a young woman traveling with the group, and she finished another quilt that she called "The Rising Sun." This quilt no longer exits, but its name alone is a symbol of hope, given her circumstances. That winter Dorinda's first grandchild, Mary Dorinda, was born at the fort on November 15, 1853, to Eliza and Robert Lloyd.

By spring of 1854 many of the pioneers were recovered and ready to set out again. Several members of the Texas group formed a small company of thirty to fifty wagons and traveled on to Utah under the leadership of Washington Jolley. Robert, Eliza, and their infant daughter went with this company while Dorinda, William, and their children stayed behind, planning to follow later.

The stop at Cherokee Nation was to be temporary, but the Preston Thomas Company stayed at the fort almost three years. Henry Miller, a missionary, who had been sent to the Cherokee Nation Mission to teach the Mormon gospel, spent a great deal of time with this company to which Dorinda and her family belonged. Many of Miller's diary entries mention the Slades, who often invited him to spend the night at their house, for

Fredonia

Dorinda's sixth daughter, Fredonia Melissa, married another Pine Valley settler, Thomas Robert Forsyth, in 1863 when she was eighteen years old. Fredonia and Robert farmed for a short time in Santa Clara but returned to Pine Valley three years later, where they lived until 1883 and where most of their twelve children were born. Fredonia and her family spent many hours visiting with Dorinda, whose home was two blocks north of the Forsyth's. Her sisters were also nearby: Eliza lived just around the corner, while her younger sister, Louisa, lived two blocks west.

The Forsyths moved to the high country near the Fremont River in central Utah in 1883. Although by today's standards the distance from Pine Valley was not great, it was a difficult trip over rugged, mountainous country, and it is unlikely that Dorinda and Fredonia met again in their lives other than the one visit in 1892 when Fredonia returned to Pine Valley with her youngest children. Fredonia's eleventh child, the then seven-year-old, Fredonia Melissa, later recalled that on this visit her eighty-four-year-old grandmother, Dorinda Slade, put the Sunburst quilt on the frame and that it took her six weeks to complete the quilting.

In Rabbit Valley the Forsyths farmed, and Fredonia and her daughters had a profitable business selling homemade cheese. As her mother and sisters had, Fredonia sewed the clothing for all of her twelve children, and from homespun wool she knitted their stockings, socks, mittens, and caps.

Information courtesy of Mrs. Hazel Forsyth Judd Gronning.
Photo courtesy of Juanita Taft Rogers.

Louisa

Louisa Jane, Dorinda's seventh daughter, married Benjamin Brown in 1864 when she was seventeen years old. Benjamin worked at a Pine Valley sawmill for six years; then the family moved eighty miles away to Panaca, Nevada, where he managed another sawmill and raised cattle. Louisa spent a great deal of time at her mother's home in Pine Valley, and although the Browns eventually resettled there, they were called by the church in 1880 to help colonize in Arizona and establish a sawmill there. After acquiring a herd of cattle and machinery for the sawmill in trade for their Utah land, they joined a wagon train of Saints traveling to Arizona. It was a sad parting. Dorinda had helped Louisa with the births of her children and had developed a special fondness for her six granddaughters. Louisa and Dorinda had spent many companionable hours together at the quilting frame. The Wheel of Fortune quilt was the last quilt they worked on together, although Dorinda sent several tops and completed quilts with the Browns on their trip to Arizona. Those quilts would have provided bedding for many years until the family could get established. Dorinda also sent with the Browns a keepsake quilt for each of her granddaughters. Because of the distance of over 400 miles and the rugged trail to Arizona, Louisa saw her mother only one more time before Dorinda's death.

The Browns arrived in Nutrioso, Arizona, in 1881, where, in addition to running the sawmill, Benjamin served as bishop of the Nutrioso church ward. The family had three more children after settling in Arizona, so their children numbered eight girls and one boy. That Louisa inherited her mother's love of flowers was evidenced in the yard around her home, which was filled each spring with masses of flowering plants.

Photo from *The John Wyatt Moody Family: Past and Present.*
Permission to reproduce photo granted by E. Grant Moody.

Victory Quilt, c. 1861.

The Victory quilt was made to commemorate Abraham Lincoln's election as president. After its completion, Dorinda gave it to her oldest stepson, William Slade, who later passed it on to his daughter Alice. Family lore recounts that it was made of cotton fabric that Dorinda had spun, woven, and dyed. The yellow dye she used was less fast than the indigo, and over the years it has faded away, leaving blue vines and blue leaves on the appliquéd border. The four wheels in each of the larger blocks have stuffed, orange centers, one-half inch in diameter. These tiny, stuffed centers appear on many of Dorinda's later quilts. In the white rectangular blocks set between the larger, pieced blocks, Dorinda quilted a lovely, original design consisting of feathered plumes and a chained edging.

Quilt courtesy of Sharon Ahlstrom. Photo by Busath Photography, Salt Lake City, Utah.

At an elevation of nearly 7,000 feet, Pine Valley is a lovely, isolated mountain village in southwestern Utah. When Dorinda and William came here in 1857 there were fewer than ten families in the valley. William built a log house near the banks of Spring Branch Creek, where Dorinda lived for nearly four decades of her life.

he had no permanent home while he traveled and preached throughout the mission territory. One entry mentions William's being chosen to head the Cherokee Branch of the church:

> July 17, 1855, Tuesday. Held meeting at Bro. Croft's and baptized four, namely: George Crouch, George Hawley and wife and Wm. Hawley and organized a branch of the church, called the Cherokee Branch and set Wm. Slade apart to preside over it; ordained 4 elders and 2 teachers. A good spirit prevailed. I preached and taught the Saints as the spirit directed. The meeting held till 11 o'clock at night.[5]

Entries continue:

> July 23, 1855, Monday. Went to Bro. Slade's. Stayed all night.
>
> July 26, 1855, Thursday. Returned to Bro. Slade's. Stayed all night.
>
> August 13, 1855, Monday. Baptized three of Bro. Slade's children and confirmed them and blessed one.
>
> April 17, 1856, Thursday. At Bro. Slade's making ax handles.[6]

While some members of the wagon train did go to Utah in 1854, many others stayed on in the Cherokee Nation for two more years. Dorinda's and William's reason for staying was never recorded, but perhaps it was William's having been named to preside over the Cherokee Branch of the Mormon church. A call from church authorities would have been a responsibility the Slades would have accepted, given their commitment to the church, even though it meant a delay in their mutual plan of moving to Utah. Early summer of 1856 found the company making preparations to journey on. Miller's diary notes:

> June 2, 1856, Monday. At Bro. Crofts . . . I found that they were ready to start for Utah.
>
> June 3, 1856, Tuesday. Went to the camp where Bro. Slade and others had driven and camped ready for a start.
>
> June 22, 1856, Sunday. Had meeting and organized the company electing Bro. Jacob Croft, Captain, Bro. Wm. Slade, Chaplain, Bro. John Hawley, Sergeant of the Guards; and Bro. S. A. Duggens, Clerk. The company consisted of 65 souls all bound for Utah.[7]

The Preston Thomas Company of "immigrating Saints" from Texas arrived in Salt Lake City on September 17, 1856. Probably within a matter of days Dorinda would have been greeted with the news of her mother's death, unquestionably a terrible disappointment. Dorinda and William went to Fort Harriman, south of Salt Lake City, where Dorinda's daughter Eliza and her husband, Robert, were living. In the spring of 1857 Dorinda's family had barely settled in when they were called to join twenty-eight families, one of them Robert's and Eliza's, sent to colonize what is today southwest Utah as part of the Cotton Mission.

Just before this departure for southern Utah, Dorinda and William were remarried and sealed in the Endowment House in Salt Lake City on April 2, 1857. Before construction of the temples, Mormon marriages took place in the Endowment House, a specially consecrated building in Salt Lake City, where the bride and groom were ceremonially sealed to each other not just until death, but for eternity. A crucial part of Mormon doctrine is that when a couple is married in the temple ceremony, or, previous to its construction, in the Endowment House, that couple will be sealed to each other forever with an "eternal ordinance." There are, additionally, special ceremonies to seal children and other family members eternally in the sacred bonds of family in order that in heaven all of the family will be together. For Dorinda and William the sealing in the Endowment House may have marked a renewed commitment to their faith and to the new lives they and their families would build together in Utah.

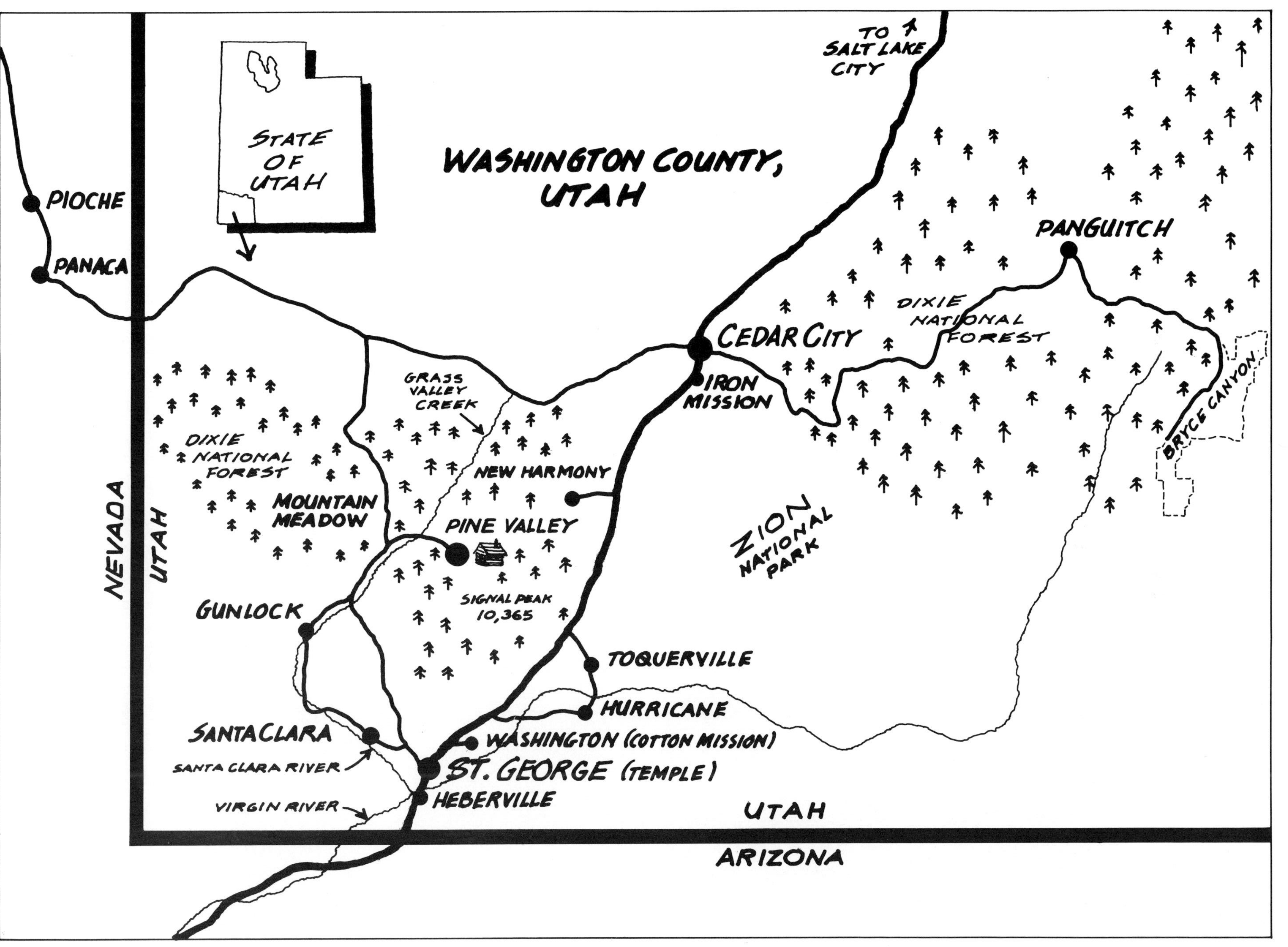
WASHINGTON COUNTY, UTAH
STATE OF UTAH
TO SALT LAKE CITY
PIOCHE
PANACA
NEVADA
UTAH
CEDAR CITY
IRON MISSION
PANGUITCH
DIXIE NATIONAL FOREST
BRYCE CANYON
DIXIE NATIONAL FOREST
GRASS VALLEY CREEK
NEW HARMONY
MOUNTAIN MEADOW
PINE VALLEY
SIGNAL PEAK 10,365
ZION NATIONAL PARK
GUNLOCK
TOQUERVILLE
HURRICANE
SANTA CLARA
WASHINGTON (COTTON MISSION)
SANTA CLARA RIVER
ST. GEORGE (TEMPLE)
HEBERVILLE
VIRGIN RIVER
UTAH
ARIZONA

Dorinda's four-room cabin in Pine Valley c. 1960. Made of sawed logs, the cabin had fireplaces in the two front rooms that shared a huge, adobe brick chimney. Behind the house the Slades planted an apple orchard, and in the front yard Dorinda grew roses and other flowering plants and shrubs.
Photo by Stanley Jay Beckstrom.

Pine Valley Years

Dorinda, her family, and many of the other Texas converts were part of a plan for the Mormon church. Brigham Young, the dynamic and charismatic second president of the church and governor of Utah Territory, led the first group of Mormon settlers into the uninhabited Salt Lake Valley only ten years earlier in 1847. As more converts arrived, they became part of Young's grand vision for the Empire of Deseret, the name by which Mormons referred to the Great Basin region, which extended south to the Colorado River, north to the Columbia River watershed, east to the Rocky Mountains, and west to the Sierra Nevadas. This vast desert empire, a territory that was described in *I Was Called to Dixie* by Andrew Karl Larson as comprising one-sixth of the total area of the United States, was envisioned as a place where the Saints could live and thrive, away from the persecutions they had suffered back East. Very important in Brigham Young's grand plan was not only settlement of this huge church-state, but also attainment of economic and material independence for his religion-based empire. As converts arrived in Utah, they were sent, according to their skills, to work and colonize the huge territory. Brigham Young was able to ask for such great obedience and sacrifice from the Latter-day Saints because they recognized that their survival in this harsh new land depended on working for the general welfare rather than personal ambition. Further, Brigham Young was a great deal more than president of the church; he was considered by the Mormon people to be their prophet and "revelator," the earthly being through whom God communicated.

While the South grew restless over the issue of slavery, the interruption of all cotton production was anticipated. Suddenly, cotton growing became vital for the survival and economic prosperity of the Saints in Utah. Brigham Young had been told of a "semitropical" climate in the area 300 miles southwest of Salt Lake City. In 1855, missionaries sent to work with the Indians near Santa Clara Creek planted cottonseed and raised enough of the crop to produce thirty yards of fabric.[8] Consequently, at the General Conference of the church in April 1857, twenty-eight families, new converts to Mormonism recently arrived from Texas, were sent to settle in Washington, Utah, along the Virgin River. Their instructions were to "supply the territory with cotton."[9]

Slade barn across the road from Dorinda's house.

Many of the first twenty-eight families were members of the Preston Thomas Company, and Dorinda's family was among those sent to "Utah's Dixie." Even though Dorinda was eager to serve her church, it was a heart-wrenching call she was asked to answer. She had already given up so much just to travel to Utah, selling her comfortable home and property in Texas and leaving behind three daughters and her husband in Texas graves. Then came the hard journey and the loss of her son, Michael, and William's three children in Cherokee Nation. Finally, news of her mother's death must have added another measure of sorrow to her staggering losses. All this was a tremendous price to pay for living near the center of her newly chosen religion. And now Dorinda was being sent away to a remote desert outpost.

In the following years as more people were asked to settle in Dixie, such calls were considered a test of faith, and although most of those called did go, it was often with great reluctance. Their disinclination came from the harsh nature of this new land. Indians in the area were hostile. The country was arid, hot, and treeless with little rainfall and alkaline soil. The Virgin River, the main drainage, had a quicksand bottom, and flash floods were common. This made agricultural ventures very difficult. Either there was not enough water or there was too much, with huge winter snow melts and flash floods washing through the dams. Between 1857 and 1859 the dam at Washington washed out seven times.[10] Malaria was also common along the river settlements, taking its toll in illness and death. In the early years, just to meet life's necessities and raise enough food to survive was a tremendous struggle. This was the area where Dorinda and William arrived in 1857 after a difficult journey over rough roads and down the treacherous Washington dugway, which led to the Dixie valley. Washington County encompassed much of the southwest corner of present-day Utah, but in the 1800s it also extended into the Arizona strip, the region north of the Colorado River, and the Nevada mining towns of Pioche and Panaca to the west. The land along the Virgin River drainage and Santa Clara Creek was considered best for cotton growing. In the center of this region in the town of Washington, the Rio Virgin Manufacturing Company, the cotton mill, would later be constructed on a tiny tributary of the Virgin River.

Without forests to supply lumber, early homes in the valley were very primitive, generally with dirt floors, gnarled cedar log walls, and willow branches with dirt for roofing, which often collapsed in the violent rains. There was a near catastrophe when Robert's and Eliza's house collapsed

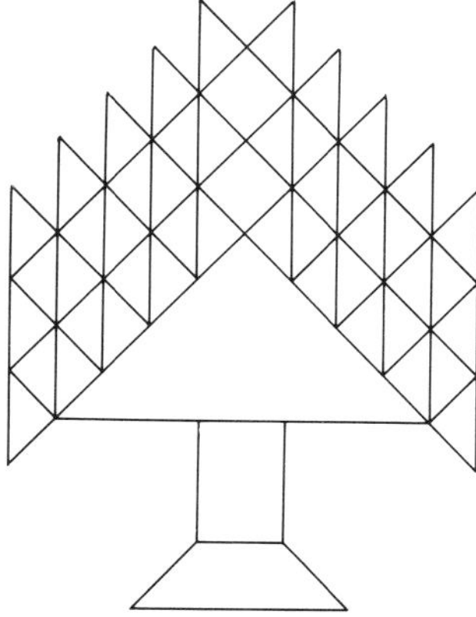

one morning, pinning Robert and their two babies under the weight of the wood and dirt. Eliza, cooking breakfast out in the kitchen lean-to, escaped being trapped. She called to the neighbors for help, and together they dug Robert and the children out. Mary Dorinda, their three-year-old, burned her arm in the fireplace, but she and the others quickly recovered from the accident.

Then, after the skies cleared, the burning sun heated the barren ground to fierce temperatures. Because shoes were almost a luxury in this newly settled country, most young children and many of the adult settlers went barefoot to spare precious materials. Descendants of those pioneers relate stories about people carrying an apron or strips of old cloth to throw down to walk on when they had to go outdoors because the ground was searing. There are tales of horribly blistered feet when someone ran across the ground without shoes or some sort of protection. Dorinda's youngest daughter, Louisa, went barefoot like the other young children. When she had to go across the yard from the house to the fields, she threw her sunbonnet ahead of her, ran, and stood on her bonnet until her feet cooled, and in this manner got across the burning dirt without blistering her feet.

We know little about the Slade home in Washington, but it is probable that this is the area where William began working as a freighter. William's and Dorinda's stay in the low country was less than a year because they were asked by the church to move once again. Thirty miles to the northeast was a lovely, green valley nestled among the pine-covered mountains. Once the Pine Valley sawmills began supplying the country with lumber, William's skills as a freighter would be of greater use there than in the Virgin River area. By the spring of 1858, Dorinda and William had moved to their last home in Pine Valley, Utah, gladly leaving behind the formidable climate of Washington.

According to Bessie Snow's history, *Oh Ye Mountains High*, the first mention of Pine Valley comes in the summer of 1855 by two Mormon cowboys in charge of herding the mission cattle, which had been driven up to the higher summer range. They discovered there a high, lush green valley with year-round streams. This valley is surrounded by the heavily timbered Pine Valley Mountains, now a wilderness area, rising 8,000 to 10,000 feet.

A sawmill was erected the year following their discovery of the valley, and it was soon followed by several others. For a time during the 1870s there were seven lumber mills operating in Pine Valley. Given the scarcity of lumber down in the agricultural areas, Pine Valley was extremely valuable as the source of wood for most of the homes and buildings in the Washington County towns and also for the mining areas to the west in Nevada. On May 12, 1863, the following description by Lyman O. Littlefield appeared in the *Deseret News*: "Pine Valley is a delightful place. It bounds in large pines of easy access. The hills in almost every direction are covered with pines and cedars and in some places there are groves down to the level land where teams can pass through them without obstruction."[11] He goes on to describe the existing structures, one of which may have belonged to Dorinda: "There are twelve dwellings here with one good sawmill in operation and two more being built. A shingle machine is nearly completed."[12] Finally, Littlefield summarizes and defines the mission's purpose: "Grass is abundant and the soil and water is excellent; but not much will be done here in agriculture, as the design of this mission is to furnish lumber for building the new locations of the Cotton Mission."[13]

Washington Cotton Mill, c. 1870.
Appleton M. Harmon was superintendent of the mill, and James Davidson, a convert from Wales, trained local women and girls in weaving the fabric. *Under Dixie Sun*, edited by Hazel Bradshaw, listed the following 1872 prices on manufactured fabrics at the mill: *Jeans $1.00 per yard; Red and Black Tweed $.90 per yard; Purple and Black Linsey $.85 per yard; Black and White Flannel $.80 per yard*. Cotton batting was 30 to 40 cents per pound and cotton yarn was $3.00 a bunch.
From the Lynne Clark Collection, St. George, Utah.

As Littlefield noted, lumber was the focus of existence for Pine Valley. Since the only road between Pine Valley and the towns to the southeast was an indirect circle route north or south around the Pine Valley Mountains, a flume was built to float logs over the mountain and down to Washington. From there the logs were hauled to a turning mill in St. George. This magnificent lumber was put to many uses. Some huge yellow pines, for example, were turned to great pipes for the organ in the Mormon Tabernacle at Salt Lake City.

The move to the lovely, isolated Pine Valley in 1857 or the spring of 1858 was Dorinda's last. She was forty-nine years old, and the small log house that she and William built was to be her home for the nearly forty remaining years of her life. Her house consisted of four rooms, with an adobe brick fireplace in each of the two front rooms, which shared a common chimney. Later, a summer kitchen was built in back of the house. The large iron kettle that Dorinda brought with her from Texas hung from an iron crane in the fireplace, where it heated water for kitchen and cleaning use. Dorinda loved flowers, and her front yard was in bloom all summer, especially with her favorites: hollyhocks and sweet peas. The yard was hedged on the north side by a bank of yellow rose bushes.

Rose of Sharon Quilt, c. 1869.

Dorinda made the Rose of Sharon quilt top for the marriage of her stepson Henry in 1869 to Amanda Burgess. The Rose of Sharon is traditionally a marriage quilt, but Dorinda's rose blocks are unusual in that they are pieced rather than appliquéd. Another interesting feature of the roses are the tiny, orange, stuffed centers. Most rose quilt blocks have larger centers, but her small, stuffed centers are a unique "signature" that Dorinda used in many of her flower motifs.

Quilt courtesy of Jan Davis. Photo by Portraits by Revoir, Provo, Utah.

Rose of Sharon quilt block detail. Pieced rose with stuffed orange center and chain-stitched stems.
Quilt courtesy of Jan Davis. Photo by Portraits by Revoir, Provo, Utah.

The hard physical work of this new frontier left Dorinda undaunted. She was a tiny woman, neat and compact, and seemed to have boundless reserves of energy. Once, when a granddaughter, commenting about herself, said she felt lazy, Dorinda scolded her severely saying, "You can say you are tired from working hard, but never let me hear you say you just feel lazy." Dorinda said she always tried to "be honest, never be idle and never put off doing tomorrow what you could do today."[14] There was a wise and direct look in Dorinda's dark eyes, but there was also a spark of fun gleaming in them. She loved music and was a superb dancer. One of the very early structures built in Pine Valley was an open-air dance floor where Dorinda and her brother John often performed for the people who came to the socials from miles around. John and Dorinda were considered the best dancers in Dixie.[15] In contrast to the toil-worn matron she might have been, Dorinda seemed to have been full of zest for life, even giving informal dancing lessons to the neighborhood children.

Dorinda wore skirts that were wide and full. In fact, many Mormon women apparently considered anything less than four full widths of fabric immodest. Her fitted basque buttoned up the front and was finished with one of her handmade, white, lace collars, and the shirt's full, long sleeves buttoned at the wrists of her slightly long arms. She generally wore a white cap with a row of double box pleats across the front. Her Sunday outfit included a dress made of black alpaca, a matching bonnet with a quilted brim, and around her shoulders, a black shawl edged with a wide, silk fringe. Though the colors would seem very severe to the modern eye, the quality and workmanship would have distinguished her at that time.

All of Dorinda's clothes were made by hand, including those for her family. And, of course, all the stitching on her quilts was done by hand. She considered sewing machines something only lazy people used. In fact, the sewing machine was not patented until 1846 and was not in common use until the mid-1860s.[16] Thus, the first half of Dorinda's life had passed before the sewing machine became available. Consequently, during her early years in Alabama, and later on the Texas frontier, hand construction of clothing and other household items, as well as fabric production, would

Pine Valley congregation, c. 1870. Photo courtesy of Bessie Snow.

have been a way of life. Of course, much of the hand sewing for Dorinda's large family on her Texas farm would have been done by slaves and servants, but in Utah the work of weaving and sewing for the Slade family would have fallen to Dorinda. It must also be remembered that Dorinda was again, as in Texas, living on a remote frontier, isolated by topography and distance from many nineteenth-century trends and products. By the time sewing machines were introduced to southwestern Utah, Dorinda was an old woman without a family to provide for, so she continued to do as she had for decades, sewing her clothing by hand. Some factory-sewn clothing was available through the cotton mill, but the costs of those items were fairly high, and for the struggling colonizers of this Mormon outpost most goods were obtained through barter while cash was saved for necessities that could not be home produced. As for Dorinda's quiltmaking, a sewing machine would not improve the quality of Dorinda's quilts. Stitching curves and tiny points can be more accurately done by hand than by machine, and for appliqué only hand sewing can achieve the tiny, hidden stitches that distinguish the finest work.

Like most quilters, Dorinda was a "saver." She saved all her fabric and scraps, even the tiniest bits if they were big enough to "cover a dime." Too many hours of tedious work went into the production of fabric to allow even the smallest pieces to go to waste. Dorinda was involved in the making of fabric throughout her life even though in the industrialized east, factory-produced cotton fabric was becoming increasingly affordable and available. Beginning with her first coverlet, made back in Alabama, Dorinda spun and wove the bulk of the fabric that ultimately went into her quilts.

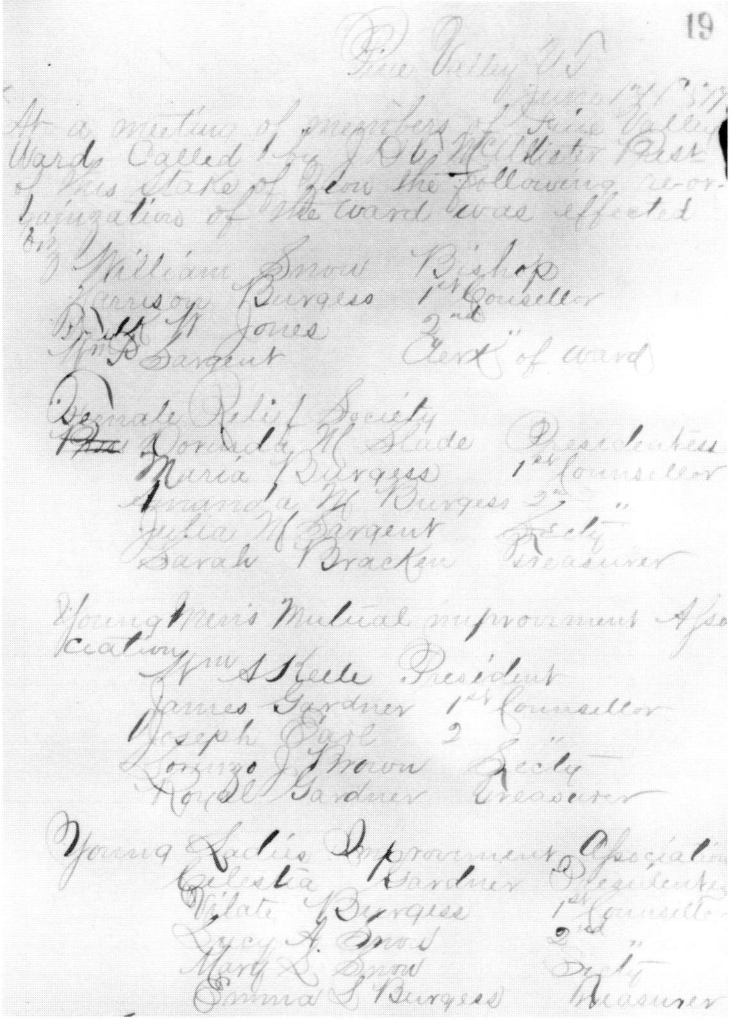
19

Pine Valley U T

June 17 1877

At a meeting of members of Pine Valley Ward Called by J D T McAllister Prest of this Stake of Zion the following re-organization of the ward was effected

viz William Snow Bishop
Harrison Burgess 1st Counsellor
Wm H Jones 2nd "
Wm B Sargent Clerk of ward

Female Relief Society
Dorinda M Slade Presidentess
Maria J Burgess 1st Counsellor
Amanda M Burgess 2nd "
Julia M Sargent Secty
Sarah Bracken Treasurer

Young Men's Mutual improvement Association
Wm A Keele President
James Gardner 1st Counsellor
Joseph Earl 2 "
Lorenzo J Brown Secty
Royal Gardner Treasurer

Young Ladies Improvement Association
Celestia Gardner Presidentess
Vilate Burgess 1st Counsellor
Lucy A Snow 2nd "
Mary L Snow Secty
Emma L Burgess Treasurer

Pine Valley Ward records, Pine Valley, Utah Territory, June 17, 1877.
Pine Valley membership records list officers of the "Female Relief Society" with Dorinda M. Slade presiding as "Presidentess." Dorinda was second president of the Pine Valley Relief Society, an office she held for twenty-one years.

Though the arts of spinning and weaving have long been a part of popular pioneer lore, the reality is that by the 1830s, homespun cotton had become very scarce. With the advent of the cotton gin and the development of the cotton spinning industry in America, factory yarn became widely available to American housewives. Quilt historian Barbara Brackman writes, "Homespun cotton is largely an American myth," although handweaving of cotton continued for some time to be common practice.[17] Brackman notes that there were exceptions in regions of the country where women continued to produce their own cotton fabric, and, indeed, both regions are areas where Dorinda lived. Brackman points out: "In the southeast where cotton grew easily, self-sufficient plantations manufactured fabric from field to clothing."[18] Certainly this practice would have been common on the cotton farms in Alabama where Dorinda passed the first decades of her life.

The other region where women continued with home production of fabric long after it was commonly available in the eastern United States was on the Texas frontier, another area where Dorinda lived. Brackman writes, "In cotton-producing frontier areas like Texas, factory cloth, cheap in the industrialized east by the 1840s, was so difficult and expensive to obtain that pioneer housewives grew, spun and wove their own cotton fabric."[19] A third region could be added to Brackman's list of areas where

Rose of Sharon Quilt.
Dorinda made the Rose of Sharon quilt top for her stepson William, possibly as early as 1864 on the occasion of his marriage to Nancy Holt. Slade family history recounts that the quilt top was made of "cotton milled in the Dixie Cotton Mission." While Rose of Sharon quilts traditionally are appliquéd, Dorinda's roses are hand pieced and feature her tiny, orange, stuffed centers.
Quilt courtesy of Marion Snow.

housewives were manufacturing cotton fabric. That region is Utah's "Dixie," settled mainly by Texas converts sent to southern Utah specifically because they had previous success raising cotton and producing cotton fabric.

After the move to Pine Valley, Dorinda was never again involved in raising cotton, which could be grown only in the low, dry country along the Virgin River drainage. It was, however, still necessary to spin and weave the cotton lint into fabric, and Dorinda and her daughter Eliza, who stayed in Washington to grow cotton, continued spinning and weaving for many years. Even though a cotton mill was built in Washington, it did not reach full production until the mid-1870s, nearly twenty years after Dorinda's arrival in Washington County.

In addition to spinning cotton for fabric, Dorinda used much of her homespun thread for lace making. Beautiful lace collars adorned her dresses and fine lace edgings trimmed her household linens. She was accomplished also at netting curtains, tablecloths, and other large lace pieces.

Detail of Rose of Sharon quilt.

While it is difficult to determine for certain whether a particular fabric has been homespun and handwoven, there are many indications, backed by recorded Moody family histories, that Dorinda's quilts were made of cotton that she had grown, spun, and woven. Furthermore, they were hand dyed, as shown by her earliest surviving quilts. Easiest to discern are blue pieces in the vine border of the Victory quilt (c. 1861), the pine tree lattice pieces in Sunrise in the Pines (c. 1866), and the Pine Tree quilt (c. 1880). Because there was no natural green dye available for home use throughout much of the 1800s, fabric was first dyed blue and then overdyed with yellow to achieve green. Indigo, for the blue coloring, was grown in southwestern Utah, and cedar berries were gathered for yellow dye. Other sources for coloring were mountain mahogany for dark brown, madder root for deep red to purple shades, and dogberry for bright red and pink.[20] The yellow dye Dorinda used was apparently fugitive or less fast than the blue and through the years has faded away, leaving her quilts today with blue vines, leaves, and trees. Dorinda made at least two Pine Tree quilts. Marjorie Ransom's Pine Tree quilt top was pieced by Dorinda before 1880, at which time her youngest daughter, Louisa, took it with her when she moved to Arizona Territory. The Ransom Pine Tree quilt top was quilted years later in Arizona by a great-granddaughter.

Dorinda's second Pine Tree quilt was used and worn out years ago. The great-granddaughter, Ida Pectol, who recalled seeing it in her mother's home, stated it was identical to the first except that the pine trees were green. Perhaps that quilt was made later with commercially dyed green fabric that was colorfast. Another explanation might be that decades earlier when Ida saw the quilt as a child, the green in her mother's Pine Tree quilt had only begun to fade to blue and still appeared to be green. Dorinda's later quilts were often pieced of factory cloth as it became more available to her. The two Sunburst quilts show what she could do with the variety of prints and colors available in commercial fabric. One has vibrant green vines, leaves, and borders, and the other is pieced with small, calico prints, which would have been easily obtainable by the late 1800s.

Stonecutters preparing blocks for the St. George Temple.
From the Lynne Clark Collection, St. George, Utah.

The St. George Temple, the first Mormon temple built in Utah, was begun in 1871 and took six years to complete. Here workers are putting on the finishing layers of plaster and whitewash.
From the Lynne Clark Collection, St. George, Utah.

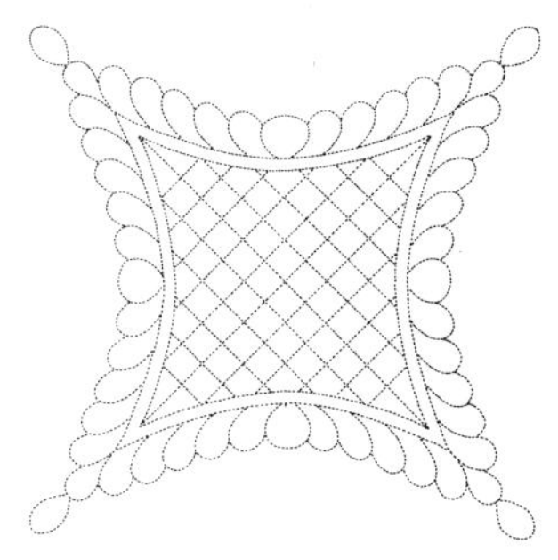

Dorinda also continued to make utility, or everyday, quilts that were much plainer than her special ones. Most of them had to be closely quilted, however, because the loose cotton filler would shift and lump unless closely stitched. When Dorinda's quilts are held up to the light and examined, small bits of hulls, bark, and leaves are visible in the batting. This is typical of many antique quilts with cotton batting, even when the batt was commercially produced. These little bits of dark matter are not cotton seeds, which are the size of a pea. Rather, these are bits of plant debris commonly found in the cotton fiber and extremely difficult to remove completely.

To make filler for a quilt, Dorinda would clean and card her cotton filler and lay it down evenly on the quilt lining in small sections. Then she would lay down her pieced top, securing it to the edges of the wooden quilt frame with pins or basting stitches. The last step was to quilt the three layers together close enough to hold the batting in place and, in the process, to stitch in a pattern that would enhance the overall design of the quilt. With a pencil or a soap sliver, Dorinda drew her quilting designs freehand, or she traced small objects such as coins or jar lids for circles and curves to form lovely, original patterns of hearts, chains, feathered plumes, flowers, and geometrics. Marking a quilt demanded skill and precision, and intricate designs such as the ones Dorinda used on her Sunburst quilts could take as many as four or five days to draw out on the quilt top. Dorinda's hardwood quilting frames were suspended from the ceiling of her front room. When she finished quilting for the day, the quilt would be covered with a sheet to protect it from dust and raised up to the ceiling and out of the way. She made many group quilts with the Women's Relief Society, the Mormon women's organization, but she did not allow anyone to work with her on her special quilts.

Dorinda obtained ideas for her quilts from her own creative mind and from the trees, plants, and natural objects around her. She always kept a notebook and pencil on the table next to her bed. When a quilt design occurred to her, she would light her coal-oil lamp and draw out the design.[21] One quilt that many people in her family tell about is the Window Pane quilt made in the winter of 1892 or 1893. Arising one snowy morning, Dorinda saw a pattern in the frost on her window. From that inspiration she created an original quilting design, which she worked on an all-white, one piece (or whole-cloth) quilt. Unfortunately, the location of that quilt is now unknown, and we are left only to imagine its beauty.

Pine Valley winters played a major role in the isolation of the tiny village and were a powerful force to be reckoned with. At an average elevation of almost 7,000 feet, Pine Valley is the second highest town in Utah. Winters there are noted for the biting cold and massive snows. Again and again through the long winter months, roads out of the valley became impassable because of heavy snowfalls, and townspeople were cut off from any communication with surrounding towns.

It is neither uncommon nor accidental that all or part of the motifs of Dorinda's quilts were original designs. The isolation of Pine Valley may have played a role in her originality since her work was created in a near void, without the stimulation artists derive when they are able to share ideas and methods. But, more important than the isolation of her valley was Dorinda's own artistic urge, which compelled her to devote much of her life to the art of her quiltmaking. It is especially impressive to view her quilts today knowing of the tremendous hardships of her life, the many

Sunburst Quilt, 81¾″ x 90″, c. 1892.

The Sunburst quilt was made by Dorinda in 1892 when she was eighty-four years old and is a stunning example of her talents in design and quiltmaking. Each Sunburst block, made of more than 200 pieces, contains four sunburst motifs composed of forty-six tiny triangles pieced into a curve. To set off the striking geometric design of the center blocks, Dorinda appliquéd an intricate and graceful rambling vine border. It took her six weeks to complete the quilting. Two years after Dorinda's death the Sunburst quilt won a first prize at the 1897 Pioneer Jubilee Fair commemorating the fiftieth anniversary of the Saints' arrival in Utah.

Quilt courtesy of Donna Shurtleff Hanson. Photo by Intermountain Films & Video Productions, Idaho Falls, Idaho.

Sunburst quilt detail.

Quilt courtesy of Donna Shurtleff Hanson. Photo by Intermountain Film & Video Productions, Idaho Falls, Idaho.

children she mothered, and the always grinding work involved in building a frontier home. Her accomplishment is nothing less than stunning.

Dorinda's quilts tend to become more elaborate through the years as the demands on her time lessened. Her hand-drawn quilting designs become increasingly complicated, and the quilts are more intricate and finely quilted. Dorinda loved borders, and she became an expert at executing beautifully flowing flowered vine borders that perfectly turned the corners and were embellished with a variety of leaves, flowers, acorns, and cherries. Just as she excelled in design and appliqué work, Dorinda also had an exceptional talent for drafting and piecing tiny points and set-in curves, which can be seen in her Sunrise in the Pines and Sunburst quilts. The sawtooth and sunburst effects are created through the use of repetitions of twelve or more tiny triangles pieced into a curve. These are quiltmaking techniques that only the most skilled needleworker could successfully attempt.

Some of Dorinda's quilts are reminiscent of patterns and styles that were popular in the east during the early 1800s. Dorinda may have seen these quilts and drawn on them as inspiration for her own work. However, after she settled in Pine Valley and was cut off from exposure to new trends in quiltmaking, she used her memories of the old patterns to create original new versions for her own quilts. Although the basic design of the Sunrise in the Pines quilt is similar to the New York Beauty or Rocky Mountain Road, in Barbara Brackman's *Encyclopedia of Pieced Quilt Patterns*, Dorinda is given credit as originator of the sunrise version.[22] To Dorinda, the Sunrise in the Pines quilt suggested the early morning sun shining through the pine trees. In *Texas Quilts, Texas Treasures*, a review of the history of quiltmaking traditions in Texas by the Texas Heritage Quilt Society, it was noted that a surprisingly large number of New York Beauty quilts were documented during their research. This was commented on because the New York Beauty is a very complex design, with an average of 2,200 to 2,700 pieces required for the quilt top, including many tiny, pieced triangles set into a curve. It was surmised that Texas quiltmakers enjoyed the challenge and an opportunity to show off their sewing prowess. Dorinda would have fit very well into this Texas tradition, as her New York Beauty variation, the Sunrise in the Pines quilt, contains more than 3,400 pieces.

Silk Culture Society

In keeping with his "gospel of economic self-sufficiency," President Brigham Young urged his people to plant mulberry trees and make their own silk for home consumption. In *I Was Called to Dixie*, Andrew Karl Larson quotes an 1872 speech in which President Young said, "If we profess to know how to use silk dresses, we should first learn how to produce them."

Silk culture became a moderately popular and successful venture for Mormon housewives in Washington County in the 1870s. Silkworms were shipped to southern Utah, and attics became silk farms as the women tended to the worms and children gathered mulberry leaves for the ravenous creatures. As described in *Under Dixie Sun* it took two and a half months of nearly constant feeding and care before the worm spun its silk cocoon of long filaments averaging 500 to 800 yards. The cocoons chosen for the silk making were dropped in hot water to kill the chrysalis and soften the glue bonding the filaments. With a small whisk broom the cocoons were turned to find an end thread. Depending on the weight of thread desired, three to fifteen threads were reeled onto a bobbin, which was then ready to be threaded onto the loom.

For a quarter of a century, enterprising Washington County women raised silkworms and produced small handwoven quantities of the prized fabric. Lack of capital to purchase looms and machinery ultimately doomed the silk culture industry in southern Utah as foreign-produced silk became more accessible and affordable.

From the Lynne Clark Collection, St. George, Utah.

Dorinda seems to have been unconcerned with artistic fashion, fearlessly using old styles in new ways. Although a quiltmaking style such as the whole-cloth quilt may have fallen out of favor in mainstream quilting, Dorinda used the whitework technique to create her Window Pane quilt decades after it had ceased to be popular in the East. Another quilt block pattern that was popular in the East before 1850 is the Whig's Defeat, which reappears, vastly modified, a half century later in one of Dorinda's last known quilts, the Hanson Sunburst quilt (c. 1892), and in the Kerr Sunburst quilt. In 1844, Democrat James K. Polk was elected to the presidency, defeating the Whig's candidate, Henry Clay. In the Kansas City Museum is a Whig's Defeat quilt dated 1844, apparently made at the time of the political event.[23] The Whig's Defeat quilt block consists of quarter-circle strips pieced with tiny, curving triangles. At the point where the curved strips meet, plumes were appliquéd, which were said to represent the tail of a rooster (at that time a Democratic party symbol). Although there are other examples of Whig's Defeat quilts made in the mid-1800s, the pattern fell into general disuse, seldom reappearing in later years. Dorinda's use of the Whig's Defeat pattern five decades later is another example, not only of her isolation from popular artistic trends, but, more important, of her ability to call upon her creative resources to overcome the limitations of her isolation. In the Kerr Sunburst quilt the pieced block has been expanded to twenty-two inches to include the four sunbursts, a delightful example of Dorinda's genius for design and pattern drafting as well as, of course, her skill in the actual stitching of the tiny pieces. This block also has the plumes appliquéd in each corner. For the Hanson Sunburst quilt, Dorinda took her block design even further, expanding it to twenty-seven inches and adding a second ring of triangles framing each sunburst. In this block the plumes are abandoned and replaced by a gracefully stylized appliqué flower and leaves at each corner. With the quilt's patchwork lattice strips and marvelously executed wandering vine border added, it is doubtful that anyone but a quilting expert could recognize the underlying characteristics of the quilt block as the Whig's Defeat.

The Whig's Defeat quilt block pattern with her original variations was probably a favorite of Dorinda's, because she made at least one other version of the Whig's Defeat quilt. In 1893, when she was eighty-five years old, Dorinda sent a Whig's Defeat quilt to be exhibited in the Chicago World's Fair. Not only did she receive a blue ribbon for her quilt, but she was also awarded what at that time would have been a grand sum of fifty dollars. When the Whig's Defeat quilt was returned from the fair it was exhibited in the Utah State Capitol Building in Salt Lake City. In the mid-1930s the quilt was borrowed for display by a San Francisco museum at the San Francisco World's Fair. Lula Crosby recalls visiting the fair and described her amazement at realizing that the magnificent quilt she was viewing in the museum exhibit had been made by her great-great-grandmother, Dorinda Moody Slade. The San Francisco museum is the last known location of the quilt.

During the early years in Pine Valley, William and Dorinda were occupied with building their home and helping to build the town. Still a remote mountain island, Pine Valley was listed in an 1860 census as having only forty-three permanent inhabitants: ten men, eight women, and twenty-five children under fourteen years of age. In spite of the fact that the arduous move from Texas to Salt Lake City and then on to southern

Utah would have been a severe drain on William's and Dorinda's financial resources, the census records their personal and real estate assets at $1,850.00, an amount comfortable for the time and place. William's work as a freighter and lumberman would have been very much in demand, a factor accounting for increases in their property over their Texas holdings.

The Slades planted an apple orchard behind the house and eventually, when William hauled lumber to the surrounding towns, the apples became an important cash crop for the family. The large herd of Texas longhorn cattle Dorinda had brought to southern Utah grazed in the nearby mountain valleys, and the huge capital **G** for Goheen was one of the earliest brands used in the area.[24] Across the road in front of the house, William built a barn for the family milk cows. A corral, a chicken coop, and an area for a garden were also constructed near the barn. In 1859 William was elected justice of the peace of Pine Valley. He also served as a school trustee, selectman of Washington County, and, for a time, as second counselor in the Pine Valley church ward.

Dorinda's earliest known surviving quilt was made in the first years after her arrival in Pine Valley. Called the Victory quilt, it was made to commemorate Abraham Lincoln's election as president in 1861. Like many women of her day, Dorinda made quilts to document the noteworthy events of her world. Although nineteenth-century women were generally excluded from politics, their quilts survive today as lasting evidence of their various political persuasions. One could possibly surmise from the number of Whig's Defeat quilts she made that Dorinda most likely leaned toward the ideals of the Democratic political party. The Victory quilt is remarkable in that it represents a complete shift in ideals on Dorinda's part from earlier days when she owned slaves to a time when she celebrated the election of the man responsible for ending slavery in America. Seen in this light, the Victory quilt contains a powerful ideological statement in fabric.

The design of the Victory quilt is less balanced than other quilts that Dorinda made. Its twelve blocks of four spoked wheels give the quilt a heavy feeling and a weighted appearance, and the motif seems incongruous with the delicately flowing appliqué border. But on close inspection, the quilt is seen to contain other features characteristic of Dorinda's stitching skills. Each wheel block is set between a rectangular white block quilted in a charming plume and chain motif. At the

Possibly the same trunk that carried Dorinda's quilts and linens across the plains to Utah nearly 140 years ago, this hand-built trunk still sits in the Pine Valley Church. For decades it was the repository for Relief Society quilting projects and held patterns and quilt blocks that Dorinda had made. It is still referred to by the few remaining Pine Valley women as "Sister Slade's trunk."

Photo by Jeffrey Gordon Rogers, with special thanks to Mitzie Rogers.

intersection of the four quilted, rectangular blocks, which may be oversized lattice pieces, is a circular, appliquéd, pieced block, made of a red circle surrounded by a pieced diamond border. While this block is suggestive of a sunflower, contemporary quilters would know it as a Dinner Plate or Cart Wheel quilt block. There can be little doubt about the Victory quilt's commentary on the times. Its flaws, if they can be called that, only reveal more clearly the ways Dorinda continued to grow as artisan and artist.

The population around the cotton mill in Washington steadily increased as the Mormon church continued to send families into the region, making the Cotton Mission prosper. In 1861, 300 more families were called to "Utah's Dixie" to raise cotton, and 200 families were added the following year. During the 1860s nearly 800 families were sent to the Washington County area as part of the Cotton Mission.[25] Much of the cotton raised in the region in the early years was shipped east or to Brigham Young's Cotton and Woolen Factory in Parley's Canyon near Salt Lake City. This factory operated for only two years, 1864 and 1865, before it was dismantled and the machinery for carding and spinning sent to Washington, Utah. There on the banks of Machine Creek, a three-story stone structure was erected to house the machinery, but various delays prevented the Rio Virgin Manufacturing Company beginning full production until the early 1870s.

For several years Robert and Eliza Lloyd lived in Pine Valley during the summers and in Washington raising cotton for the mission during the winters. Robert was elected Washington County assessor and tax collector. Eliza, a talented and competent person in her own right, spoke Piute and was often asked to serve as an interpreter in dealings between her Mormon neighbors and the Indians. She and Robert had a family of twelve children, nine of whom grew to adulthood. Raising so large a family was a feat that then, as now, required tremendous energy and managerial skills. As part of the household tasks, Eliza made carpets of long cloth strips sewn together and woven to room size. Fresh straw was spread on the floor for padding, and the carpet was laid over it, stretched to the edges of the room, and tacked down. Laying the carpet became an annual chore, as each year when the hay was cut the carpet was taken up and aired and fresh straw was laid down. Eliza's carpets were sold and made to order to supplement the household income. From the cotton she and Robert raised, Eliza made all the cloth for her family's needs. Although all of Dorinda's daughters were capable needlewomen and quiltmakers, none of them seemed to inherit the love of quilting and the spark of creative drive that Dorinda had. Eliza, however, was an excellent weaver. And even though most of her work commonly went for utilitarian purposes in the form of clothing and linens for her large family, her love for the craft compelled her to continue spinning and weaving long after fabric and factory clothing were easily available. During Eliza's early years in Washington, cotton was gathered by hand, cleaned, and carded. With the whole family helping, about one pound of cotton could be cleaned in an evening. Eliza spun cotton yarn on the small spinning wheel Robert had purchased for her, and until she had better spindles, she wound the yarn onto corn cobs. She owned a company loom, and the river supplied reed cane for bobbins.[26]

This charming scene shows several of Dorinda's great-grandnieces sewing and reading outside of their Penrose, Wyoming, tent home in 1919. The sisters have dressed for the occasion of having their photograph taken; note the flowers worn in their hair and as necklaces.
Photo courtesy of Ireta Shurtz.

Many other Washington housewives spun and wove the cotton that their families raised. Spinning bees were regularly held in homes where women could bring their spinning wheels and baskets of cotton, and as they spun the lint into yarn, they could socialize and catch up on community events. Often when the work was done the women were joined by the men, and together they enjoyed a "rattlin' good dance."[27]

Dorinda's brothers, John and William, were among the converts sent to Dixie as part of the Cotton Mission. For a time after their arrival in Utah, John and his wife, Margaret, lived in Salt Lake City with their daughter, Mary Ann, and Margaret's three sons from a previous marriage. On January 23, 1856, with the consent of his first wife, John took a second wife, eighteen-year-old Elizabeth Pool. Elizabeth wrote in her journal, "We lived in the same house, cooked and ate at the same table, but set up in separate rooms."[28]

Polygamy or "celestial marriage" was a central part of the early Mormon church doctrine. It was introduced by Joseph Smith, founder of the church, through a revelation in the mid-1830s and was likened to the polygamous marriages of the early prophets in the Old Testament. In spite of the notoriety it brought to the Mormons, polygamy was never widely practiced among church members. Rather, it was the custom of only a small group of church leaders and their hand-picked representatives in the community. During the half century when polygamy was practiced, approximately a fifth of the church population lived in polygamous families.[29] A man took more "spiritual wives" only on the recommendation of church leaders and then, generally, only with the approval of his first wife.

Shortly after John Moody's second marriage, he and his brother William were called by church leaders to go to Texas for missionary work, to teach the gospel of the Latter-day Saints. They returned to Texas and began the work of making converts. Among the people they met and converted were the Damrons, a family with two young daughters, twenty-year-old Cynthia Elizabeth and twenty-one-year-old Sarah Matilda. John married Sarah, and William married Cynthia in the same ceremony in the Endowment House in Salt Lake City on December 20, 1857, each sister becoming her husband's third wife.

John Monroe Moody
1822-1884.

When John was called to "Dixie" he was an elected member of the legislative assembly of the territory. He settled his first wife, Margaret, in a home in Washington and his two younger, pregnant wives near Dorinda in a vacant house in Pine Valley. He then returned to Salt Lake City to finish his 1860 term with the legislature. At the end of that year, John returned to southern Utah and bought a farm in St. George, where he settled his families. John served as school trustee, justice of the peace, and alderman in St. George. When construction of the Mormon Temple was begun in 1871, John worked on it one day a week, donating a day of labor as partial tithing, along with fellow members of the School of the Prophets until the temples' completion in 1877.

In 1878, fifty-eight-year-old John Moody married his fourth and last wife, eighteen-year-old Margaret Lenora Pace. This was the year following the death of Brigham Young, second president of the church, and that year marked a growing public focus on Mormon polygamy. After the Civil War, national attention increasingly turned to Utah, since most of the nation viewed polygamy as the last vestige of female slavery in America. In 1878 the United States Supreme Court upheld the 1862 antipolygamy statute. Federal deputies raided Mormon communities, arresting known polygamists, confiscating church property, and excluding Mormon voters from the polls. Polygamists and their families went into hiding or fled the territory to western Canada, Arizona Territory, and northern Mexico. In 1881, John Moody, with his second and fourth wives, traveled to eastern Arizona as part of this general exodus of polygamous families who were fleeing prosecution by the federal government. The family settled in Smithville, one of the small Mormon farming communities along the Gila River.[30]

William Cresfield Moody
1819-1906.

Dorinda's brother William had also settled in southern Utah after doing missionary work in Texas and England. He had arrived in Utah in 1853 with his wife of thirteen years, Harriet, and their five children. When William entered into "celestial marriage" on December 20, 1857, he took a second wife, Lola Eliza Bess, as well as a third wife, the Damron girl, Cynthia Elizabeth. Both girls were twenty years old.[31] William worked as a brick and stone mason in Salt Lake City. His skills resulted in a call by church authorities in 1863 to relocate in St. George. Three years later, William and his families were again called to move, this time to Eagle Valley, Nevada, where William presided over a branch of the church. Before leaving St. George, William married a fourth wife, Louisa Gillard Williams. Six years later in 1872, William married Victoria Regina Rogers, his fifth and last wife.[32]

With persecution and arrest of polygamists escalating in the 1880s, William fled to Arizona Territory in 1885 as had his brother, John, before him. William settled in the Gila River Valley near other Mormon colonies. In her wagon hauled over the rugged Arizona trail, Louisa, William's fourth wife, carried the Sunrise in the Pines quilt, the wedding gift given to her almost two decades earlier by her sister-in-law, Dorinda Slade. Louisa Moody claimed in later years that her two most treasured possessions were a set of Blue Willow dishes brought with her from England in 1865, and the Sunrise in the Pines quilt.

Wheel of Fortune Quilt, c. 1880.
When the Brown family received a call to settle in Arizona, Louisa and her mother spent their remaining hours together stitching the Wheel of Fortune quilt. Louisa pieced the top and Dorinda marked the hearts and plumes quilting pattern. Together, mother and daughter quilted the Wheel of Fortune quilt before it was packed into the wagon that would carry them away from Pine Valley to a new home in Arizona Territory.
Quilt courtesy of Janie Hobson.

Mines opening in Pioche, Nevada, then a part of Utah Territory, created further demand for lumber, and more people moved into Pine Valley. At one time the population of the town reached almost 600. Most of that number were mill hands, however, and Mormon church membership in the Pine Valley Ward peaked at 275.[33]

A combined church-schoolhouse was built in 1868 in Pine Valley under the direction of Ebenezer Bryce, an Australian shipbuilder and Mormon convert for whom Bryce Canyon National Park was later named. The church, built with hand-hewn pine logs and set together with auger holes and wooden pins, is modeled, according to townspeople, on an inverted hull of a ship, a construction form that Bryce would have been most familiar with. Dorinda's son-in-law Robert Lloyd built a lime kiln and made the plaster for the church interior. The Pine Valley Chapel stands today as the oldest continuously used church in Utah. In addition to serving as a chapel and school, the building was also used as a social hall. Community dances were held there, and a local dramatic company performed plays on the church stage every winter.

As in every Latter-day Saint church ward after 1867, the Pine Valley ward also had an active Female Relief Society, the official organization of women within the church. The Relief Society women conducted welfare projects, raising funds and gathering food, clothing, and quilts to help the poor and sick. They built many of the buildings where they met, supported the Silk Culture Society and built granaries to store wheat for food or seed. Their official publication, *Woman's Exponent*, was a bimonthly paper with a woman editor, women writers, and women contributors.[34]

Dorinda was elected president of the Female Relief Society on April 1, 1873, a position she held for twenty-one years, until September 16, 1894, when she resigned at the age of eighty-six because of failing health. Under her direction the Relief Society built a granary to store wheat. The granary stood well into the twentieth century. During World War II as part of the

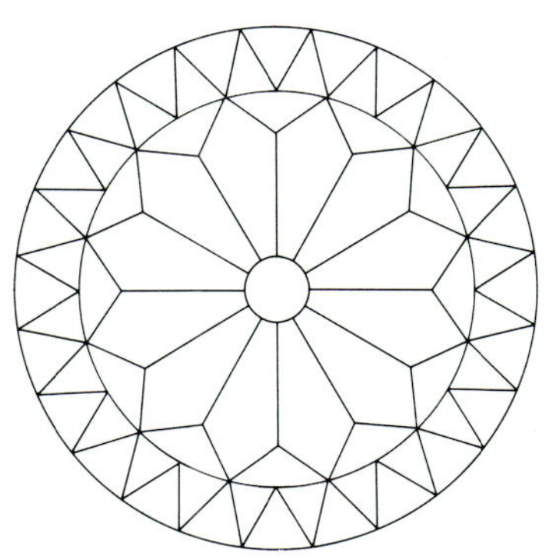

Detail of Wheel of Fortune quilt.

Wheat Fund for the war effort, the women of the Relief Society gleaned and thrashed wheat and stored it in the granary until it could be shipped out to Salt Lake City.

Another important activity of the Relief Society was making quilts for community members and service projects. One central Utah Relief Society Stake, an organization combining several local societies, reported that in two years members had made and donated 504 quilts.[35] A tiny community such as Pine Valley certainly could not contribute as many quilts, but the ladies did their share of sewing, meeting regularly at the church or in homes to stitch on the group quilts. Often when such a quilt was on the frame in a Relief Society member's home, neighbor women would come by throughout the day to sit and quilt for whatever length of time they could contribute, often without the presence of the hostess, who was expected to continue with her daily work. Under Dorinda's direction many group quilts were created by the Relief Society sisters. A hand-built wooden trunk, perhaps the same one that Dorinda brought in her wagon from Texas, still sits in the Pine Valley Chapel and is referred to even today as "Sister Slade's trunk" by the few remaining inhabitants of Pine Valley. This trunk was the repository for Relief Society materials, notably the fabric, patterns, and sewing supplies for the Relief Society quilts. Until many decades after her death, the trunk also contained quilt blocks that Dorinda had pieced.

By 1870, after thirteen years in Pine Valley, the rigors of daily life lightened for William and Dorinda. Demand for lumber was high and William, with two of his married sons, had a brisk business hauling wood from the sawmills to the mines in Panaca and the booming towns in Washington County. All of their children were now living on their own. William and Henry Slade lived in Pine Valley, as did Dorinda's daughters and their families, except for Christiana and her husband, who settled in Panguitch, Utah.

The last of their children's marriages had taken place in the fall of 1869, when William's son, Henry, married Amanda Melissa Burgess. One of the gifts Amanda received from Dorinda was a Rose of Sharon quilt top. The Rose of Sharon was a traditional pattern for a marriage quilt, generally a best quilt saved for special occasions.[36] Like many of the quilts Dorinda

Pine Valley.

Dorinda Slade

WOMAN'S EXPONENT.

The Rights of the Women of Zion, and the Rights of the Women of all Nations.

VOL. 18. SALT LAKE CITY, UTAH, JANUARY 1, 1890. No. 15.

CONTENTS.

like her to get. It will take from now to Christmas to cook it all. I will tell her what to do. Ma wont care." "No, Hessie I am the oldest and this is my right. But we will leave it to the cook which of us shall order the dinner." Mamie hears the girls rattling away about the Christmas dinner. "I am going to settle this myself," the cook said, as she stept into the kitchen, where the girls were often found busy with domestic affairs.

"Now girls I will order: What shall it be? turkey, a fat goose, chickens and a roast."

"Lucia may make the ginger cake, a loaf of

usual walk one afternoon discussing the Christ mas tree and dinner thus.

"Dear Hess, we will hang the tree with garlands, we will take the hemlock, pine and evergreens and weave them into wreaths and twine them around the tree intermix them with the house flowers. I think we can spare some. We can make artificials also and surprise pa and ma will this not be a grand idea?" Hessie drank in all that her sister said gathered up all that her arm

"Dear sister

Copy of Dorinda's January 1, 1890, issue of the *Woman's Exponent*, the official publication of the Relief Society. *Exponent* courtesy of Pine Valley Chapel. Used by permission.

made, the Rose of Sharon pattern was most popular in the 1840s and 1850s and by the Civil War had dropped out of common use by mainstream quiltmakers in eastern cities. The name of the block comes from the Song of Solomon: "I am the rose of Sharon, and the lily of the valleys." The verses are generally recognized as celebrating the passion and love between a man and a woman and honoring the sacrament of marriage.[37] Thus, Dorinda's gift would have been her wish for happiness and love in their years to come together, as well as an indication of the maternal affection for her stepchildren that had deepened through the years.

This was not the only Rose of Sharon quilt that Dorinda made. She also gave one to her oldest stepson, William, on his marriage to Hannah Pierson in 1864. A remarkable feature of Dorinda's Rose of Sharon quilts is that, although they appear to be appliqué work, the large rose motif in the center of each block is pieced, an endeavor that would have demanded a great deal more effort and skill than the traditional appliqué. Where an appliquéd rose would require only three or four fabric pieces, each of Dorinda's pieced roses contains seventeen to twenty-five or more pieces, the pattern requiring that all the pieces be exactly fitted and stitched into a curve. In addition to the unusual piecing of her Rose of Sharon quilts, Dorinda also used a distinctive tiny orange center in each of the flowers. This center, less than one-half inch in diameter, has extra stuffing to give it more depth. This tiny, interesting detail also appears in the flowered border of the Hanson Sunburst quilt. While nineteenth-century quiltmakers made thousands of rose motif quilts, most roses were appliquéd and only a very tiny number were pieced like Dorinda's.[38]

By the sixth decade of her life and with all her children married and settled, the only dark cloud over Dorinda's life was her husband's declining

Dorinda's daily attire included a white cap with double box pleats around her face and one of her white lace collars adorning her dress.
Portrait courtesy of Aileen Butler.

health. Increasingly William was plagued with lung and breathing problems. While on a freighting trip to Panaca, William became seriously ill with tonsillitis, then known as quinsy. He died quite suddenly in the winter of 1872.[39] William was buried there in Panaca, Nevada. His sons, William and Henry, with their father's empty wagon between theirs, returned home to Pine Valley, bringing Dorinda the news of William's death. For the third time, Dorinda had lost a husband who died far from her and was buried far away without her presence.

The deaths of Dorinda's first two husbands occurred while she was still faced with the work of caring for and supporting young children. At sixty-four, widowhood must have held the daunting prospect of an old age alone with the rigors of pioneer life still before her. The Slade marriage had been a working arrangement; however, Dorinda and William did live together and care for each other for almost two decades. Although they had no children together, they were loving parents to each other's children. Even though each may have longed for their late spouses, still, together they achieved the difficult goals of building a home and a community in which they could openly practice their religion.

Although William's death did not devastate Dorinda the way, twenty-two years earlier, losing Michael had, she was now alone and much older. Undoubtedly the following years were lonely, but suffering may sometimes endow an artist with a greater clarity of vision, and time alone is an artist's

Double Squares Quilt Top. Dorinda never finished the Double Squares quilt. She hand pieced twenty blocks for the planned quilt, but they were left unfinished at her death. More than half a century later they were given to her great-granddaughter, who stitched the blocks together.
Quilt courtesy of May Mecham.

great ally. As an older woman Dorinda still had abundant creative energy, and this was channeled into her quilts.

A granddaughter, relating Dorinda's domestic habits, recalled that she washed on Monday, went to Relief Society on Tuesday, ironed and mended on Wednesday, baked on Thursday, and always did her chores in the mornings so that every afternoon could be devoted to her needlework.[40] This steady schedule gave her a structured block of time to work, an aid to artistic creativity. Clearly, her art flowered in the years after William's death. Living alone and unburdened of huge family responsibilities, she was able to produce impressive quantities of lace, woven coverlets, and, of course, quilts. She was accomplished at fine crochet as well. One example of her skill in this craft is a homespun cotton crocheted bedspread, made for her neighbors the Hyrum Ozro Gardner family, also early settlers in Pine Valley. Their family kept the crocheted bedspread for many years. But it is in her quilts above all that we find Dorinda's greatest artistic achievements, with some of the most beautiful, skillfully crafted quilts coming from these last years. While some artists continue creating into their old age, it is rare that a quiltmaker is able to do so. Usually perfect eyesight and a steady hand for fine work are lost early in the aging process. Dorinda, however, never wore glasses and, apparently, was blessed with excellent eyesight her whole life. It is thus doubly impressive to look at Donna Hanson's 1892 Sunburst quilt, knowing Dorinda created it at eighty-four. Furthermore, in the following year she won the blue ribbon and fifty dollars at the Chicago World's Fair for her Whig's Defeat quilt.

By 1880, demand for lumber had fallen off, and as the mills closed people began leaving Pine Valley. Polygamist families, such as John and William Moody and their wives, were fleeing the area to avoid federal

Built in 1868 under the direction of Ebenezer Bryce, an Australian shipbuilder, the Pine Valley Church is modeled on an inverted hull of a ship. It is the oldest continuously used chapel in Utah. During the 1800s the building also served as a school and a social hall.

prosecution, and church authorities were calling on members to colonize the newly opened Arizona Territory. Dorinda's youngest daughter, Louisa, and her husband, Benjamin Brown, were among those requested by the church to colonize in Arizona. Although the Browns had lived for many years in Panaca, Nevada, where Benjamin ran a sawmill and raised cattle, Louisa spent many of the summer months each year at the cooler elevation of her mother's Pine Valley home. She also returned often to be near her mother for Dorinda's help with the births of her babies. At the time of the call to go to Arizona, the Browns had just moved back to Pine Valley, where Benjamin operated a sawmill. Church leaders requested him to move the sawmill and operation to Arizona. The Browns traded their Utah land for a herd of cattle, which they took with them, along with machinery for the sawmill. In early October they joined a wagon train of Saints and began the rugged journey into a new desert wilderness. Farewells must have been very sad, and, as it turned out, Louisa was to see her mother only once more before Dorinda died.

Tithing office located on the east side of the Pine Valley Church.

The route the Browns took to Arizona had only recently been opened. Earlier parties sent to explore the area in the 1870s had returned with reports that the land was impassable and the country too barren to support either agriculture or settlement. The 400-mile route, which later came to

be known as the Honeymoon Trail, went southeast from St. George, Utah, climbed the Buckskin Mountains, wound down through Houserock Valley, and traversed the Vermillion Cliffs. The most difficult part of the journey was the dangerous crossing of the Colorado River at Lee's Ferry. Immediately on the east side of the river was the steep, treacherous ascent several hundred feet up a rock incline, popularly known as Lee's Backbone. From this point the trail went southeast through barren desert, following the Little Colorado River, which, ironically, was often so silt-laden as to render it undrinkable, making the scarcity of potable water a major concern. The Mormon settlements were located at the eastern end of the river in Arizona and south, down the eastern edge of the state.

The route's colorful name, the Honeymoon Trail, is derived from a marriage rite unique to the Mormon faith. The honeymooners were the Arizona colonists who made the six-week round trip to Utah and back to have their marriages solemnized in the St. George Temple. Couples could be married in a civil ceremony in Arizona, but, in order to be "sealed" to a spouse for "time and all eternity," the sealing ceremony had to be performed in a Mormon temple. Groups of newlyweds gathered for the trip to Utah to be sealed. Sometimes betrothed couples invited a chaperone to accompany them back over the arduous trail to St. George, where the marriage ceremony was performed at the temple. At the height of federal prosecution in the 1880s and 1890s the trip to Utah also afforded a means of establishing polygamous marriages without leaving records in the hands of unsympathetic government agencies in Arizona.

When the settlers left Pine Valley, Louisa was seriously ill and lay on a pallet on the floor of the wagon for the entire journey. To the couple's five daughters fell the work of caring for Louisa, and while the older girls watched the youngest children, the family wagon was driven over the entire 400 miles of trail by Louisa's oldest daughter, fifteen-year-old Melissa Jane. Louisa's husband had the double responsibility of driving the cattle and overseeing the wagon carrying machinery for the sawmill.

The Browns reached Holbrook, Arizona, on Christmas Eve, and hearing of a dance being held in town, the indomitable Melissa, inheritor of her grandmother's love of dancing, put on her best dress and waltzed the night away. After the holidays the Browns went on to Snowflake, Arizona, where they spent the remainder of the winter. In spring they continued southwest to become founding settlers of the town of Nutrioso.

One cherished heirloom brought in the wagon with them was a quilt, product of Dorinda and Louisa's joint effort. Louisa pieced the Wheel of Fortune blocks and Dorinda drew out the quilting design, a four-part, feathered plume with double hearts between the plumes. When the blocks were all joined, mother and daughter quilted the Wheel of Fortune together.

It is interesting to note a "signature" of Dorinda's quilting. When she began a new quilting thread, instead of burying the knot in the batting she left the knot on the lining side of the quilt with a short tail showing. Perhaps this was a habit formed in earlier days when handwoven fabrics may have had a looser weave. Rather than chance the knots pulling through to the front of a quilt, she left them exposed on the back. Today these knots can be found on the back of every quilt Dorinda made. On Louisa's quilt the evidence of two different quilters' work appears. And where one quilter buried her knots, the other quilter left her knots exposed.

Washington Cotton Mill, c. 1928. From the Lynne Clark Collection, St. George, Utah.

The Wheel of Fortune quilt, like many others, became a tangible link between Dorinda and her family across distances and generations. To Louisa the quilt must have been a comfort and a reminder of Dorinda and Pine Valley as she struggled to build a new home in Arizona, where living conditions were primitive and communication was nearly nonexistent.

Dorinda's descendants describe quilts made for each of Dorinda's grandchildren, step-grandchildren, and many great-grandchildren. She made quilts for friends, for the church, and for her brother's extended families. With each quilt Dorinda must have known she was stitching a loving bond between herself and the recipient, and indeed, she was even creating a bond with all the succeeding recipients of her quilts down through future generations.

It is tantalizing to hear stories of these quilts. Some of them are lost forever, used up and worn out. One was given to a passing tramp because the owner's husband thought it was the most tattered, hence worthless, quilt in the house. Melissa Jane Brown carried one of her grandmother's quilts in the wagon she drove over the Honeymoon Trail in 1880. Her quilt was lost in a house fire in 1912. At the time of Eliza Lloyd's death in 1922, a trunk in her Pine Valley home was reported to contain thirty-five quilts, nine woven coverlets, and numerous pieces of lace made by Dorinda. Eliza had filled the trunk with her mother's quilts and stitchery and saved it for almost thirty years. At present, no one knows what became of the trunk or its contents. In tiny Eagar, Arizona, a town settled by the descendants of Dorinda's youngest daughter, Louisa, a quilt collector reported having seen a quilt at an estate sale that strongly resembled the Sunburst quilt, and it had "knots on the back." There are reports of one of Dorinda's quilts that the present owner will not allow anyone, family or friends, to see. It is likely that more of Dorinda's quilts exist. Sadly, it is probable that they are lost because present owners have no record of their history.

Early travelers painted their names with wagon-axle grease or chiseled them into the rock walls above Houserock Springs, leaving a fragile record that they had come this way on their long journey through this barren country.

Disappointing as it is to hear of Dorinda's lost quilts, the fact remains that for a hundred years or more almost a dozen of her quilts have survived. In them today is revealed the life of a nineteenth-century housewife and the growth of a pioneer artist through her quiltmaking. Dorinda recorded political, ideological, and religious events in fabric. Her quilts are documents of her family history; they celebrated weddings and births and heralded sorrowful partings. In a larger sense they are a great deal more than lovely heirlooms. They are chroniclers, not only of an extended family, but also of a unique era and people and the important role those people played in settling the American West.

Two years after Louisa and Benjamin left for Arizona, Dorinda's third daughter, Fredonia, and her family moved away to Thurber, Utah. The population of Pine Valley steadily declined in the twentieth century until only a handful of families remained, and the only visitors to the valley were descendants of original settlers or curious travelers exploring the ghost town. After Louisa and Fredonia's departure, the only family Dorinda had left in Pine Valley was William's son Henry, her oldest daughter, Eliza, and her son-in-law Robert Lloyd.

Dorinda continued the work of tending her home and garden. She still kept chickens. She did her Relief Society work, and, of course, she never stopped quilting. But she was increasingly troubled by thoughts of her death and the implications of her "sealing" to William Slade, three decades earlier. The Mormon religion views the hereafter as rather similar to earthly life but on a more conscious and joyous level. Families are believed to be together in heaven, existing in love and harmony. It was to insure such eternal family closeness that a marriage was sealed. Here was the dilemma. Dorinda had been sealed to William Slade, but her second husband, Michael Goheen, had always remained in her heart as the love of her life, and it was with Michael she desired to spend eternity. She went to church authorities at the temple in St. George and tried, unsuccessfully, to have her sealing to William annulled. Then, early in 1884, Mortimer Slocum, William's nephew, visited Pine Valley. Mortimer had come west to visit the long lost family of his father's brother. Strangely, Dorinda seems to have known very little about her third husband's family, Mortimer being

The Honeymoon Trail was the route early colonizers took from Utah to the Mormon settlements along the Little Colorado River. Young couples wishing to have their marriage solemnized or "sealed" made the 400-mile trip back to Utah to the St. George Temple for the sacred ceremony. Charles Peterson writes in *Take Up Your Mission* that many polygamists also traveled over the Honeymoon Trail to perform the secret rites of temple marriage. They returned to Arizona as husband and wife but left no public evidence of the event to indict themselves.

In addition to names and inscriptions left on the rock walls at springs and stopping places, wagon tracks such as these leading southeast to the Colorado River crossing are still visible on many sections of the Honeymoon Trail.

the first relative she had met. And she had never known that William Slade's real name was Washington Slocum.

Soon after Mortimer's visit, Dorinda returned to the temple in St. George, and with the information about her husband's name she was able to obtain a release from her sealing to William Slade. On March 8, 1884, on what she often referred to as "the happiest day of my life," Dorinda was sealed to Michael Roup Goheen. She was seventy-six years old. Of course, after two decades of marriage to William Slade, and as the only mother the younger Slade children had ever known, Dorinda's actions did cause some scandal and some hurt feelings, for it meant that she would not be part of their family in heaven. For Dorinda, however, the sealing to Michael gave her great peace of mind, and she took comfort in the knowledge that Michael, her dearest love, would be her companion for eternity.

As Dorinda approached her eighties she continued to be independent and productive. She carried on her work with the Relief Society, tended her flowers and the apple orchard, and put in a garden each spring. She still kept a few chickens in the barn across the road. She saw Eliza and Robert daily, often entertained her visiting grandchildren and great-grandchildren, and continued to save her afternoons for quilting and piecing new quilts. Three of her most notable quilts come from the last years of her life: the Window Pane quilt, the World's Fair quilt, and the Hanson Sunburst quilt. Her granddaughter Fredonia Melissa Forsyth recalled that when in 1892 Dorinda quilted the Hanson Sunburst quilt, it was only on the frame six weeks, an impressively short time for even an accomplished quiltmaker to finish a piece as finely and heavily quilted as the Sunburst quilt. Two years after Dorinda's death, the Sunburst was displayed in Salt Lake City at the Pioneer Jubilee Fair, celebrating the fiftieth anniversary of the Saints' arrival in Utah. The quilt won first prize.

The winter of 1894-1895 was exceptionally cold with heavy snowfall. One morning as Dorinda walked out to feed her chickens in the barn across the road, she fell and broke her left arm and hip. She never recovered. Bedridden with her broken hip for the last year of her life, Dorinda's work was at an end. On November 21, 1895, at the age of eighty-seven, Dorinda Slade died. She was buried two days later in the Pine Valley Cemetery on the hill above the church. She had survived three husbands and five children, but her headstone stands alone, a small granite marker with only the initials D.M.S.

Over the years, the population of Pine Valley steadily declined, with only a handful of permanent residents remaining. For most of the twentieth century, Pine Valley has been only a memory to the people who left for towns and jobs. The Pine Valley Chapel is open for Sunday services in the summers now that the valley has been rediscovered by a new influx of tourists and winter visitors to St. George. The log house where Dorinda lived has collapsed, and the yellow rose hedge blooms in a tangled profusion each spring.

The real memorial to Dorinda's life is not in her obscure and humble headstone. Rather, it is in the light and brilliance of her creativity, which radiates from her quilts. Dorinda must have known that she was stitching more than utilitarian bed covers. In the tiny pieced points and curves, the flamboyant borders, and delightful quilting designs, her exhilarating genius and energy can still captivate viewers nearly a century after her death. Dorinda was an artist working with a fabric palette and a quilting frame. Her quilts have become the documents of her family and events in her world. They are, ultimately, a record of the creative growth of a remarkable nineteenth-century artist.

Dorinda's headstone sits near the far wall of the Pine Valley cemetery, with only the letters D.M.S. to designate her final resting place.

WOMAN'S EXPONENT

The Rights of the Women of Zion, and the Rights of the Women of all Nations.

Vol. 24. SALT LAKE CITY, UTAH, JANUARY 1, AND 15, 1896. No. 15-16.

IN MEMORIAM.

SISTER DORINDA M. SLADE died Nov. 21st, 1895, at the residence of her daughter Eliza A. Lloyd, after a lingering illness of eight months. She fell on the ice and broke her arm on the 26th of March last, and has been confined to her bed ever since; although her arm was perfectly healed before her death.

She was born Jan. 15th, 1808, joined the church in the fall of 1850, came to Utah in 1856, moved to Dixie in 1857, and settled in Pine Valley in 1858. She was elected president of Pine Valley Relief Society, April 1st, 1873, which position she held until Sept. 16th, 1894, a period of over twenty-one years, and resigned at this time on account of failing health.

She was the mother of eight children, only three of whom are now living, but she lived to see the fifth generation of her posterity.

Dear Sister Slade has now left us; she has gone to Heaven above; it is God who has bereft us of her whom we dearly love. In the Relief Society she has been true and has worked as none but she could do. We shall miss her, yes miss her one and all; but on our Father in Heaven we must call. It is hard to part with loved ones, but God knows what is best, and we must put our trust in Him then He will do the rest. Her loved name will never perish; her good deeds we'll ever cherish. She has gone from before our face, a moment's time, a little space.

RESOLUTIONS OF RESPECT.

Resolutions of respect adopted by the officers and members of the Pine Valley Relief Society to the memory of Dorinda M. Slade.

Whereas our Heavenly Father has removed from this sphere of action, our beloved ex-president Dorinda M. Slade.

Resolved that we do recognize in the death of Sister Slade the loss of an energetic, faithful and reliable friend. A comforter in the hour of trouble, a devoted wife and mother and a true Latter-day Saint, that we esteem her faithful labors and devotion to the cause of Zion as worthy the emulation of every member of our society.

Resolved that we do sincerely sympathize with the bereaved family and friend.

Resolved that these resolutions be placed upon the records of the Pine Valley Relief Society and a copy be sent to the WOMAN'S EXPONENT.

Committee
ANN R. SNOW, President
LENORA C. GARDNER
EMMA L. BURGESS,
BERNELLA E. GARDNER.

Acknowledgments

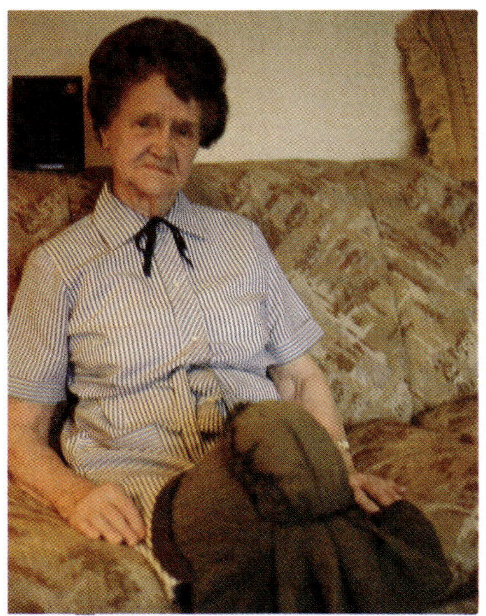

Annie Eliza Forsyth McMurtrey

Janie Eagar Hobson

Cleo May Burgess Greenwood

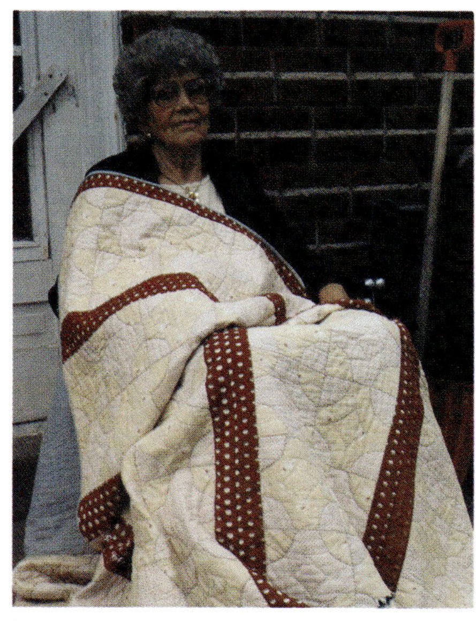

Rayola Fredonia Heilson Gibson

Fredonia Adams Shurtleff Hanson

Colleen Haycock Kerr

Zella Beckstrom Ahlstrom

May Crosby Mecham

Marian Miller Snow

Marjorie Merrill Ransom

In many respects this volume has truly been a group effort. Without the support and assistance of numerous members of the Moody family it would never have become a reality. Additionally, many experts gave advice and suggestions, and several librarians and historians were very helpful in locating information and photographs. To all of those people, and to my family and friends, I offer my deepest thanks. There were, furthermore, ten very special ladies who not only loaned their quilts and heirlooms to the project, but also gave their support and enthusiasm. Over the years their letters and visits have been a sustaining influence and their dear friendships were an unexpected bonus.

Marian Miller Snow

Marian Snow inherited twenty pieced Rose of Sharon quilt blocks and three vined border pieces, which she saved for almost thirty years. The quilted blocks were pieced by Dorinda Slade, Marian's great-grandfather's second wife, and family lore recounted that the blocks were made of "cotton milled at the Dixie Cotton Mission." The Rose of Sharon pattern is generally appliquéd, but Dorinda's quilt blocks were pieced, a more difficult and time-consuming process, which is rarely seen in nineteenth-century Rose of Sharon quilts. Marian recently had the quilt blocks set together and quilted by the Relief Society women in her church. The Rose of Sharon quilt is now prominently displayed in the entry of her daughter's home.

Janie Eagar Hobson

Janie Hobson was given the Wheel of Fortune quilt by her mother, Delila Eagar, who told her that it was pieced by her grandmother before the Brown family moved to Arizona in 1880. Dorinda marked the quilting pattern, and mother and daughter quilted it together before the long journey that would separate the families for the rest of their lives, with the exception of one visit before Dorinda's passing. Janie treasures her quilt, and although it has been used and well loved over the years, Louisa's fine piecing and Dorinda's lovely quilting designs can still be seen on the Wheel of Fortune quilt.

Marjorie Merrill Ransom

When Louisa and Benjamin Brown traveled to Arizona in 1880, they carried in their covered wagon several quilts and quilt tops that had been pieced by Louisa's mother, Dorinda Slade. The Pine Tree quilt top was one of those brought from Utah. It was not quilted by the women in the Brown family until sometime after they had resettled in Arizona. The quilt was passed on to Louisa's youngest daughter, Cordelia. After her death, it was discovered in a trunk left to her only daughter, Marjorie Ransom. The deceptively simple Pine Tree block is a lovely sample of Dorinda's fine hand piecing. Each of the twenty pieced blocks is constructed of sixty-six pieces, with all of the points and corners meeting in ordered precision.

Zella Beckstrom Ahlstrom, 1905-1990

Alice Slade Miller, granddaughter of William Slade, was a neighbor to Ella Caroline Lloyd Beckstrom when the two families lived in Panguitch, Utah, during the early 1900s. Upon discovering the link to their two ancestors, Dorinda and William Slade, Alice remarked that she owned one of Dorinda's quilts, which she felt more properly belonged to Ella's line of the family as Ella was Dorinda's granddaughter. Alice then gave the Victory quilt to her neighbor and good friend Ella Beckstrom, who carried the quilt with her on subsequent moves to northern Utah and California. Zella Ahlstrom inherited the Victory quilt after her mother's death in 1951 and with Zella's passing in 1990 the quilt has returned to Utah, 130 years after Dorinda made the quilt to commemorate Abraham Lincoln's election as president of the United States.

Cleo May Burgess Greenwood

Cleo Greenwood believes that her 1826 sampler is the best of all the keepsakes left by Dorinda, her great-grandmother. Cleo's mother, Melissa Brown Burgess, returned to Pine Valley to visit her Aunt Eliza Lloyd sometime before Eliza's death in 1922. In Eliza's home Melissa noticed the sampler, which was on a cushion on an armless rocker. When Melissa commented that the sampler had been made by her grandmother, Eliza took the sampler off the rocker and presented it to Melissa as a gift to take back to her home in Arizona. Cleo, who is now a great-grandmother herself and in her early nineties, has owned the sampler for more than forty years. Because of her lifelong interest in genealogy and family history, Cleo treasures her sampler and proudly shows it off to visitors in her northern Arizona home.

May Crosby Mecham

After the death of her youngest daughter in 1941, Christina Lloyd became very ill and was confined to her house. To help with her grandmother's recovery, May Crosby Mecham went to Salt Lake City and lived with her elderly grandparents for nine months. As a special thank-you gift for her assistance over the nine long months of healing, Christina and William Lloyd gave May twenty Double Squares quilt blocks that had been made by Dorinda Slade and passed on to her grandson William. May stitched the twenty hand-pieced blocks together and now treasures the quilt top pieced a century ago by her great-great-grandmother.

Colleen Haycock Kerr

Colleen Kerr's grandmother, Christiana Dixie Lloyd Riding, ran a hotel in Panguitch, Utah, where, on the beds, were quilts made by Christiana's grandmother, Dorinda Slade. When Colleen went to Panguitch to visit her grandmother, she always asked to sleep under the Sunburst quilt, as it was her favorite. After her grandmother's death in 1946, Colleen requested the quilt as the one keepsake from her grandmother's home. Today the Sunburst quilt is a much-loved heirloom in the Kerr family, and in spite of the years of wear, Dorinda's precise hand piecing and closely spaced quilting are still marveled at when the quilt is taken out for display.

Annie Eliza Forsyth McMurtrey, 1902-1989

Almost fifty years ago, Annie McMurtrey's father gave her the bonnet he had brought with him years earlier in the move to his Idaho farm. The bonnet, packed away in a trunk, was a keepsake that had belonged to his grandmother, Dorinda Slade, who had worn the store-bought bonnet on Sundays and for special occasions. The bonnet had special meaning for Annie, who had a life-long interest in history and had spent many years gathering information for her family's genealogical records.

Fredonia Adams Shurtleff Hanson

Fredonia (Donna) Hanson, named after her mother and grandmother, is the third "Fredonia" in her family, and although she never cared for the name she inherited (children at school called her "fried doughnuts") Donna did have the good fortune to also inherit the fabulous Sunburst quilt from her mother in 1970. Made in 1892, the Sunburst quilt was on the quilting frames for six weeks. Because it was one of the last quilts made by Dorinda, when her daughter Fredonia Forsyth took it to her home in Thurber, Utah, she kept the quilt as a keepsake from her mother and never used it as a bedcovering. After Fredonia's death the quilt was given to Fredonia Adams, her eleventh child, who took it with her to St. George, Utah, where she lived after her marriage. The quilt now belongs to the third Fredonia, Donna Hanson, who carries on the tradition of caring for the quilt and preserving it for future generations of family and quilt lovers. The stunning Sunburst quilt has been protected from damage and wear, and all the fabrics are as vivid and true as they were when Dorinda pieced them together a hundred years ago.

Rayola Fredonia Heilson Gibson

As a young bride in 1927, Rayola Gibson went to live on a ranch in Maple Canyon near Franklin, Idaho, in a one-room log house without electricity or running water. Times were hard for the young couple, and when her children were born Rayola quilted the old Snowball quilt top and used it to keep her family warm in the bitter winter months. She knew the quilt top was old – it had been hand pieced decades earlier by her great-grandmother, Dorinda Slade. Being a quilter herself, Rayola set great sentimental value in the top she had inherited. As soon as she was able to piece more quilts for her family, Rayola folded up the Snowball quilt and takes it out now only for special occasions.

Notes

1. Dorothea Kay, *Embroidered Samplers* (New York: Charles Scribners Sons, 1979), p. 81.
2. John Wyatt Moody wanted his oldest son to become a lawyer, but in 1835, when Francis was nineteen years old, they had a serious disagreement regarding his profession; Francis wanted to go into the ministry. Francis stayed in Alabama when the rest of his family moved to Texas, and he later became a Methodist preacher. He changed the spelling of his name to Moodie and had no further contact with his family after they left Alabama. See E. Grant Moody, ed., *The John Wyatt Moody Family: Past and Present* (Tempe, Ariz.: Dr. Thomas Moody Family Organization Inc., 1985), p. 379.
3. Moody, *The John Wyatt Moody Family*, p. 379.
4. The story of Angelina's tragic love was recorded by Dorinda's great-granddaughter, Orpha Cope. Coincidentally, Orpha also experienced a great sorrow when her fiancé was killed in an automobile accident shortly before their marriage. A school friend, Edna Christenson, was the plural wife of Charles Zitting. Edna introduced Orpha to her husband and, at Edna's invitation, Orpha became Charles's seventh wife in 1932 (Moody, *The John Wyatt Moody Family*, p. 161).
5. Henry William Miller, *Journal of Elder Henry William Miller, April 1855 – Spring 1862* (From the files of The Utah State Historical Society, Salt Lake City, Utah), p. 8.
6. Miller, *Journal of Elder Henry William Miller*, p. 10.
7. Miller, *Journal of Elder Henry William Miller*, p. 27.
8. Leonard J. Arrington, "The Mormon Cotton Mission in Southern Utah," *The Pacific Historical Review* 25, no. 3 (August 1956): 222.
9. Hazel Bradshaw, ed., *Under Dixie Sun: A History of Washington County by Those Who Loved Their Forebears* (Panguitch, Utah: Washington County Chapter, Daughters of Utah Pioneers, 1950), p. 63.
10. Bradshaw, *Under Dixie Sun*, p. 39.
11. Bradshaw, *Under Dixie Sun*, p. 187.
12. Bradshaw, *Under Dixie Sun*, p. 187.
13. Bradshaw, *Under Dixie Sun*, p. 187.
14. From unpublished material on the life of Dorinda Melissa Moody Slade written by her granddaughter Ella Caroline Lloyd.
15. Lloyd, unpublished history.
16. Barbara Brackman, *Clues in the Calico: A Guide to Identifying and Dating Antique Quilts* (EPM Publications, Inc., 1989), p. 20.
17. Brackman, *Clues in the Calico*, p. 38.
18. Brackman, *Clues in the Calico*, p. 38.
19. Brackman, *Clues in the Calico*, p. 39.
20. A. R. Mortensen, ed., "Utah's Dixie: The Cotton Mission," *Utah Historical Quarterly* 29, no. 3 (July 1961), 13.
21. Coal oil and kerosene lamps were the only source of light in Pine Valley homes well into the twentieth century. It was 1964 before the R.E.A. brought the first power lines into Pine Valley.
22. Barbara Brackman, *An Encyclopedia of Pieced Quilt Patterns* (Lawrence, Kans.: Prairie Flower Publishing, 1984), p. 113.
23. Barbara Brackman, "Patterns to Ponder," *Quilt World Omnibook* (Winter 1984).
24. Bess Snow and Elizabeth Beckstrom, *Oh Ye Mountains High: The Story of Pine Valley* (St. George, Utah: Heritage Press, 1980), p. 51.
25. Arrington, "The Mormon Cotton Mission in Southern Utah," p. 227.
26. Moody, *The John Wyatt Moody Family*, p. 46.
27. Moody, *The John Wyatt Moody Family*, p. 46.
28. Moody, *The John Wyatt Moody Family*, p. 541.
29. Leonard J. Arrington and Davis Bitton, *The Mormon Experience: A History of the Latter-day Saints* (New York: Alfred A. Knopf, 1979), p. 185.
30. Moody, *The John Wyatt Moody Family*, p. 538.
31. Not everyone in Dorinda's family embraced the concept of polygamy with the same apparent enthusiasm that John and William did. Ida Riding Littlefield told of a humorous incident regarding her mother, Christiana Dixie, Dorinda's granddaughter, which occurred when a Mormon Elder, Brother Weaver, came to ask for her hand in plural marriage. Christiana's mother, Eliza Lloyd, teasingly announced that Brother Weaver had come courting. Christiana looked up from the loom where she was weaving and replied, "If that old cuss comes anywhere near this door I'll throw this shuttle clear through him." Needless to say, Christiana never did become one of the Mrs. Weavers.
32. Moody, *The John Wyatt Moody Family*, p. 338.
33. Bradshaw, *Under Dixie Sun*, p. 189.
34. Arrington, *The Mormon Experience*, p. 227.
35. Arrington, *The Mormon Experience*, p. 228. A report of the Sanpete Stake Relief Society for May 19, 1879, proclaimed that over a two- to three-year period the Sanpete women had: Gathered 21,507 dozen Sunday eggs for charitable and philanthropic purposes; Made 504 quilts; Made five rugs and 3,633 yards of rag carpet; Gathered 11,093 bushels of wheat; Collected 111 books for their library; Acquired four acres of land; Manufactured 1,084 yards of cloth; Donated $5,310 to temples; Helped 399 families of missionaries, and sent off $2,925 to missionaries in the field; Made 52,550

visits to the sick; Clothed and prepared for burial 299 corpses; Built seven Relief Society halls; Held two bazaars or fairs; Built one co-op store, acquired shares in these stores and two mills and one thrasher; Made 11,199 pounds of cheese; Donated $5,965 to the emmigration fund; Spent $2,159 for surprise parties for the poor.

36. Bets Ramsey, *Old and New Quilt Patterns in the Southern Tradition* (Nashville, Tenn.: Rutledge Hill Press, 1987), p. 100.
37. Suzzy Chalfant Payne and Susan Aylsworth Murwin, *Creative American Quilting Inspired by the Bible* (Old Tappan, N.J.: Fleming H. Revell Company, 1983), p. 76.
38. Bets Ramsey, "Roses Real and Imaginary: Nineteeth-Century Botanical Quilts of the Mid-South," *Uncoverings 1986* (Mill Valley, Calif.: American Quilt Study Group, 1987), p. 20. Ramsey first noted the appearance of the pieced rose during the Tennessee quilt survey. Prior to that time, it had generally been assumed that all rose-motif quilts were constructed with the traditional appliqué technique. Of 1,425 quilts documented for the Tennessee survey, twelve pieced rose quilts were discovered.
39. It is interesting to note that while William and Dorinda had been married almost twenty years at the time of his death in 1872, the date of William's death is exactly twenty years to the day after the death of his first wife, Julia Ann, who died on November 28.
40. Lloyd, unpublished material on Dorinda Slade.

Bibliography

Arrington, Leonard J. "The Mormon Cotton Mission in Southern Utah." *The Pacific Historical Review* 25, no. 3 (August 1956): 221-38.

Arrington, Leonard J., and Davis Bitton. *The Mormon Experience, A History of the Latter-day Saints*. New York: Alfred A. Knopf, 1979.

Brackman, Barbara. *An Encyclopedia of Pieced Quilt Patterns*. Lawrence, Kans.: Prairie Flower Publishing, 1984.

Brackman, Barbara. *Clues in the Calico, A Guide to Identifying and Dating Antique Quilts*. EPM Publications, Inc., 1989.

Brackman, Barbara. "Patterns to Ponder." *Quilt World Omnibook*. Winter 1984.

Bradshaw, Hazel, ed. *Under Dixie Sun, A History of Washington County by Those Who Loved Their Forebears*. Panguitch, Utah: Washington County Chapter, Daughters of Utah Pioneers, 1950.

Bresenhan, Karoline Patterson, and Nancy O'Bryant Puentes. *Lone Stars, A Legacy of Texas Quilts, 1836-1936*. Austin, Tex.: University of Texas Press, 1986.

Carter, Kate B., ed. *Pioneer Quilts*. Salt Lake City, Utah: Daughters of Utah Pioneers, 1979.

Kay, Dorothea. *Embroidered Samplers*. New York: Charles Scribner's Sons, 1979.

Larson, Andrew Karl. *I Was Called to Dixie*. St. George, Utah: 1979.

Lloyd, Ella Caroline. Unpublished material on the life of Dorinda Melissa Moody Slade.

Miller, Henry William. *Journal of Elder Henry William Miller, April 1855 – Spring 1852*. From the files of The Utah State Historical Society, Salt Lake City, Utah.

Mortensen, A. R., ed. "Utah's Dixie: The Cotton Mission." *Utah Historical Quarterly* 29, no. 3 (July 1961).

Moody, E. Grant, ed. *The John Wyatt Moody Family: Past and Present*. Tempe, Ariz.: Dr. Thomas Moody Family Organization, Inc., 1985.

Orlofsky, Patsy, and Myron Orlofsky. *Quilts in America*. New York: McGraw-Hill, 1974.

Payne, Suzzy Chalfant, and Susan Alysworth Murwin. *Creative American Quilting Inspired by the Bible*. Old Tappan, N.J.: Fleming H. Revell Company, 1983.

Peterson, Charles S. *Take Up Your Mission, Mormon Colonizing Along the Little Colorado River, 1870-1900*. Tucson, Ariz.: The University of Arizona Press, 1973.

Ramsey, Bets. *Old and New Patterns in the Southern Tradition*. Nashville, Tenn.: Rutledge Hill Press, 1987.

Ramsey, Bets. "Roses Real and Imaginary: Nineteeth-Century Botanical Quilts of the Mid-South." *Uncoverings 1986*. Mill Valley, Calif.: American Quilt Study Group, 1987.

Snow, Bess, and Elizabeth Beckstrom. *Oh Ye Mountains High, The Story of Pine Valley*. St. George, Utah: Heritage Press, 1980.

Texas Heritage Quilt Society. *Texas Quilts, Texas Treasures*. Paducah, Ky.: American Quilter's Society, 1986.

Yabsley, Suzanne. *Texas Quilts, Texas Women*. College Station, Tex.: Texas A&M University Press, 1984.

Patterns

Piecing by hand is recommended for most of the patterns featured. The simpler patterns, such as the Pine Tree, can be pieced on the sewing machine.

Hand Piecing – Prepare templates for the patchwork patterns by tracing the patterns directly onto translucent plastic (available at quilt shops) or by tracing onto paper and pasting to poster board. Trace the inside, or sewing, line. Place the templates on the wrong side of the fabric, following the grain lines on the patterns. Mark around the templates, using a sharp pencil. Leave at least 1/2 inch between the shapes to allow for seams. Cut 1/4 inch away from the marked line.

Pin the pieces together on the sewing line. Using a small needle (either sharps or betweens), and a single strand of thread, sew with small, even stitches. Begin and end the stitching on the marked line. Do not sew over seam allowances; simply move the previously sewn seams away from the line of stitching. Press the seams to one side.

Machine Piecing – Trace the outside line of the patterns. Mark around the templates on the wrong side of the fabric, using a common line between the shapes. Cut on the marked line. Several layers of fabric can be cut together by pinning carefully.

Sew the pieces with a 1/4-inch seam allowance, either judging by eye or marking the surface of the sewing machine. Begin and end the stitching at the raw edge of the fabric. It is not necessary to backstitch. When crossing other seams, place the seams in opposite directions. This will reduce bulk and insure a better match. Press the seams to one side.

Appliqué – Trace the pattern pieces as for patchwork. Place these on the right side of the fabric, and mark with a fine line, using pencil or dressmakers' chalk pencils. Cut a scant 1/4 inch beyond this line. Prepare the background block by folding and creasing it in quarters and diagonally. Pin or baste the appliqué pieces to the background. Using the needle to turn the seam allowance under, sew with small blind stitches. (Many quilters today baste under the seam allowances first; the nineteenth-century quiltmaker simply turned them under as she stitched.) Use a fine needle (either betweens or sharps) and a single strand of matching thread.

Quilting – Trace the quilting designs onto the quilt by placing the fabric over the patterns, using a light box if necessary. Mark very lightly, with regular or chalk pencils. Quilt, using small betweens needles and quilting thread, in the traditional white or matching color. Strive for small, straight, and uniform stitches.

For complete instructions on making quilts, check your local fabric or quilt shop or library for current books on the subject.

Sunburst 27″ Block

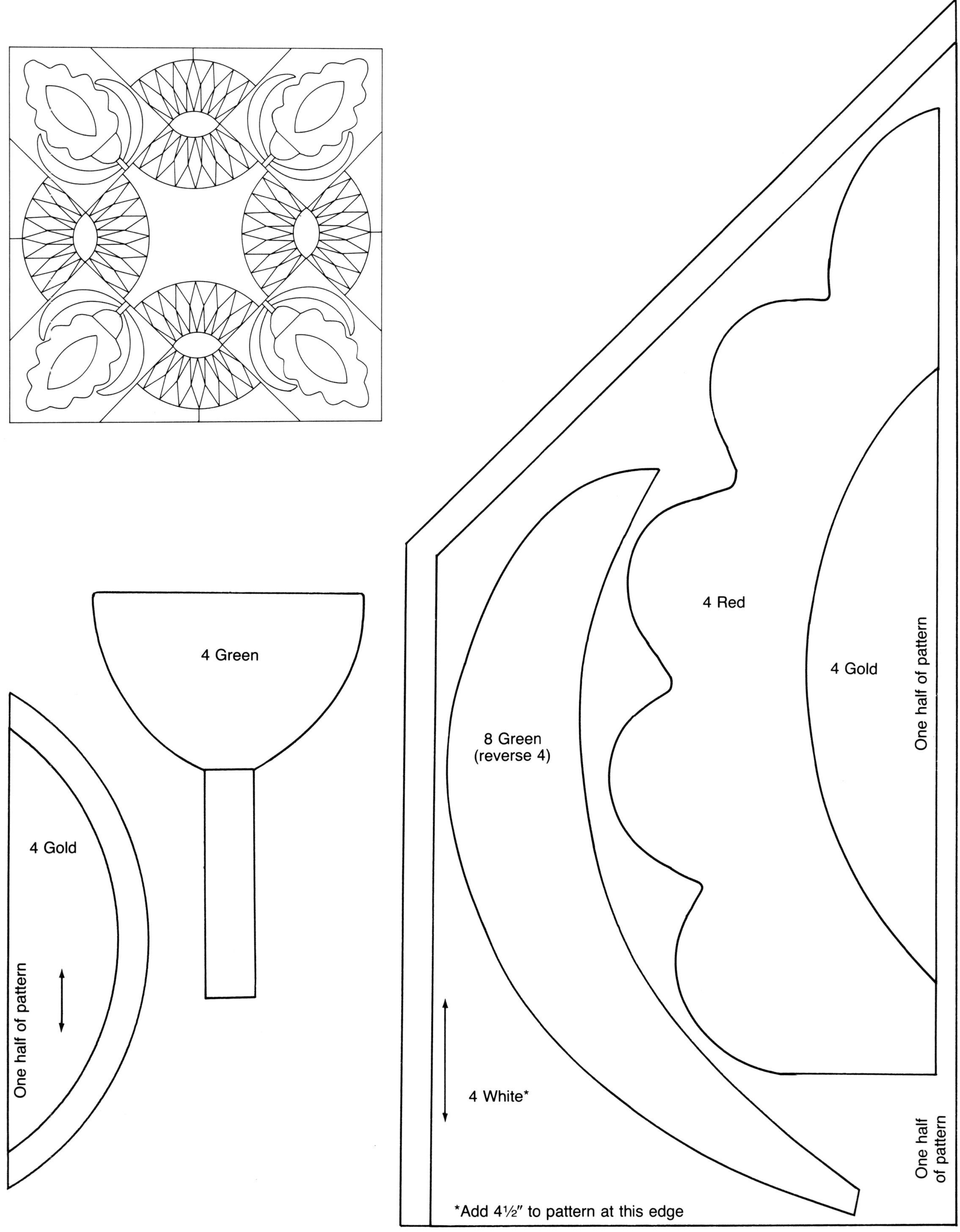

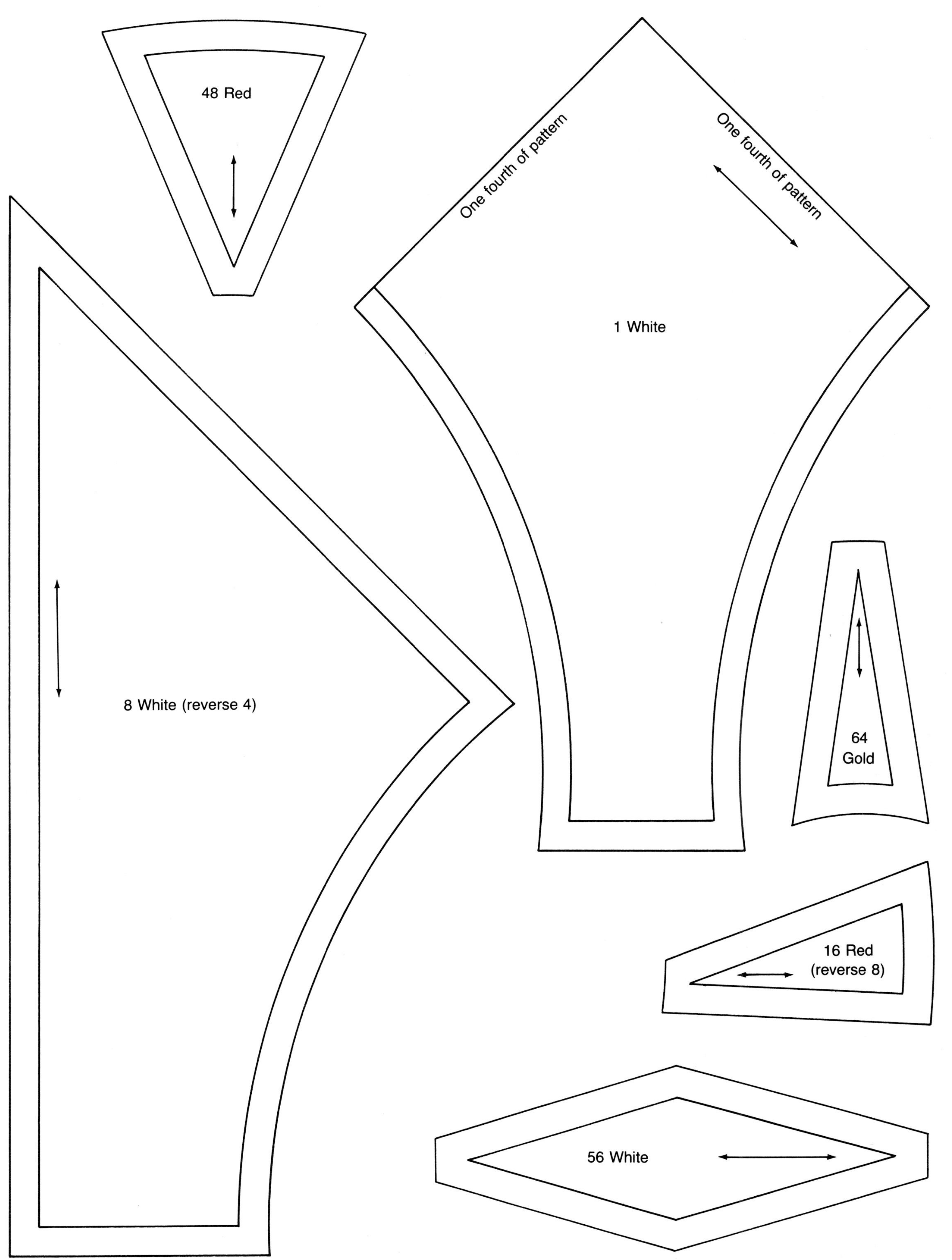
48 Red
One fourth of pattern
One fourth of pattern
1 White
8 White (reverse 4)
64
Gold
16 Red
(reverse 8)
56 White

Pine Tree 13½″ Block

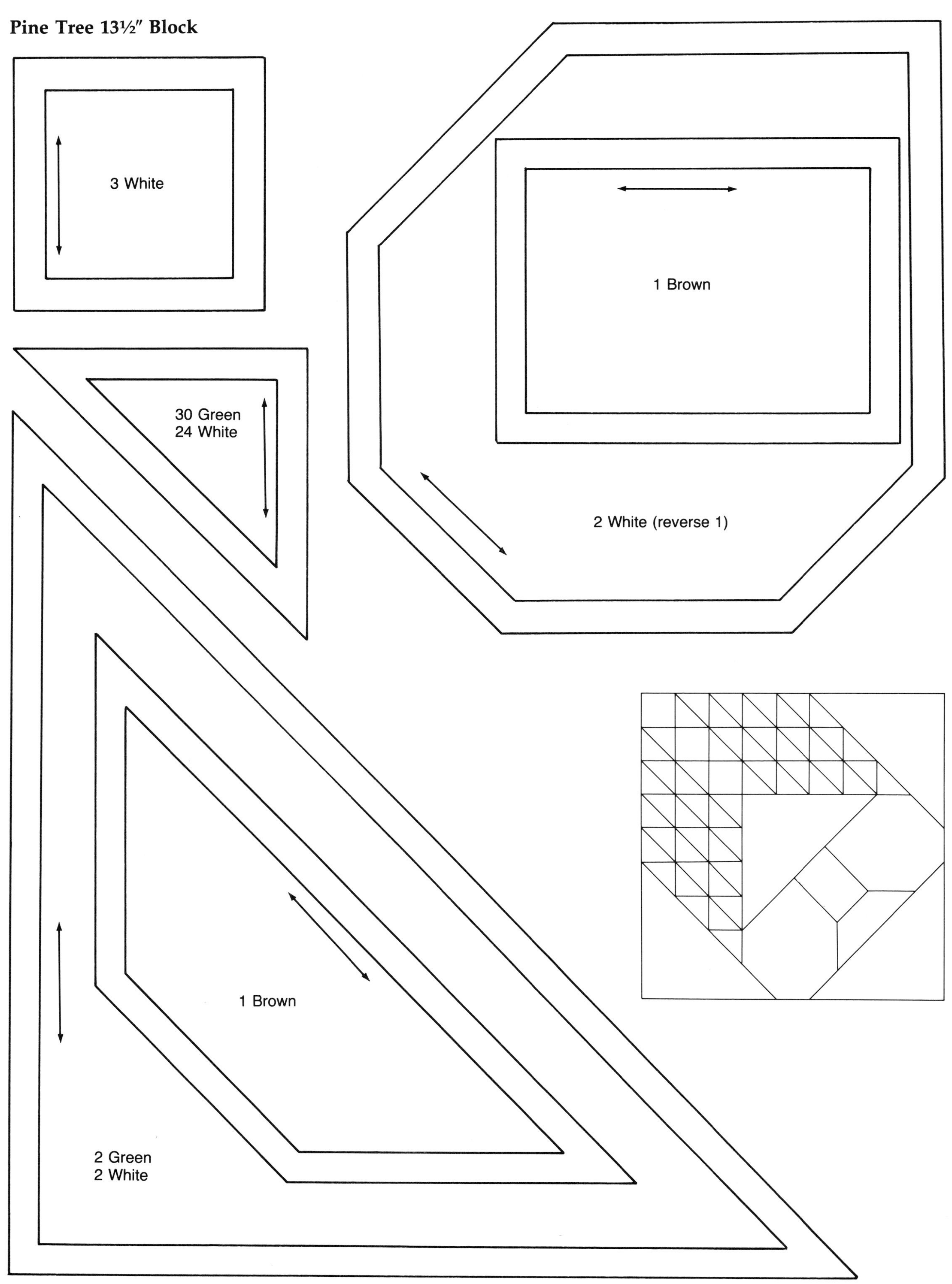

Rose of Sharon Blocks

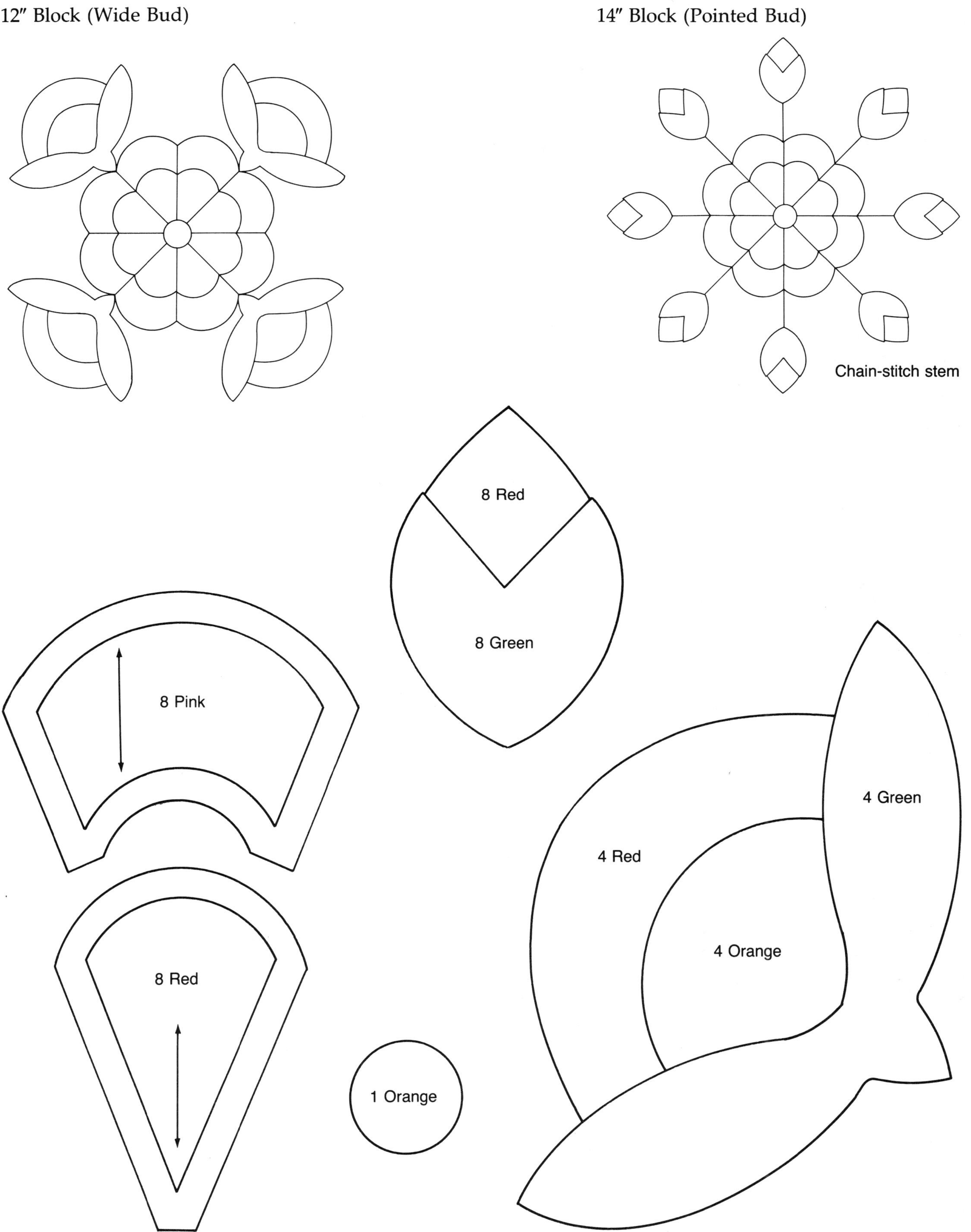

Quilting design from Wheel of Fortune Quilt.

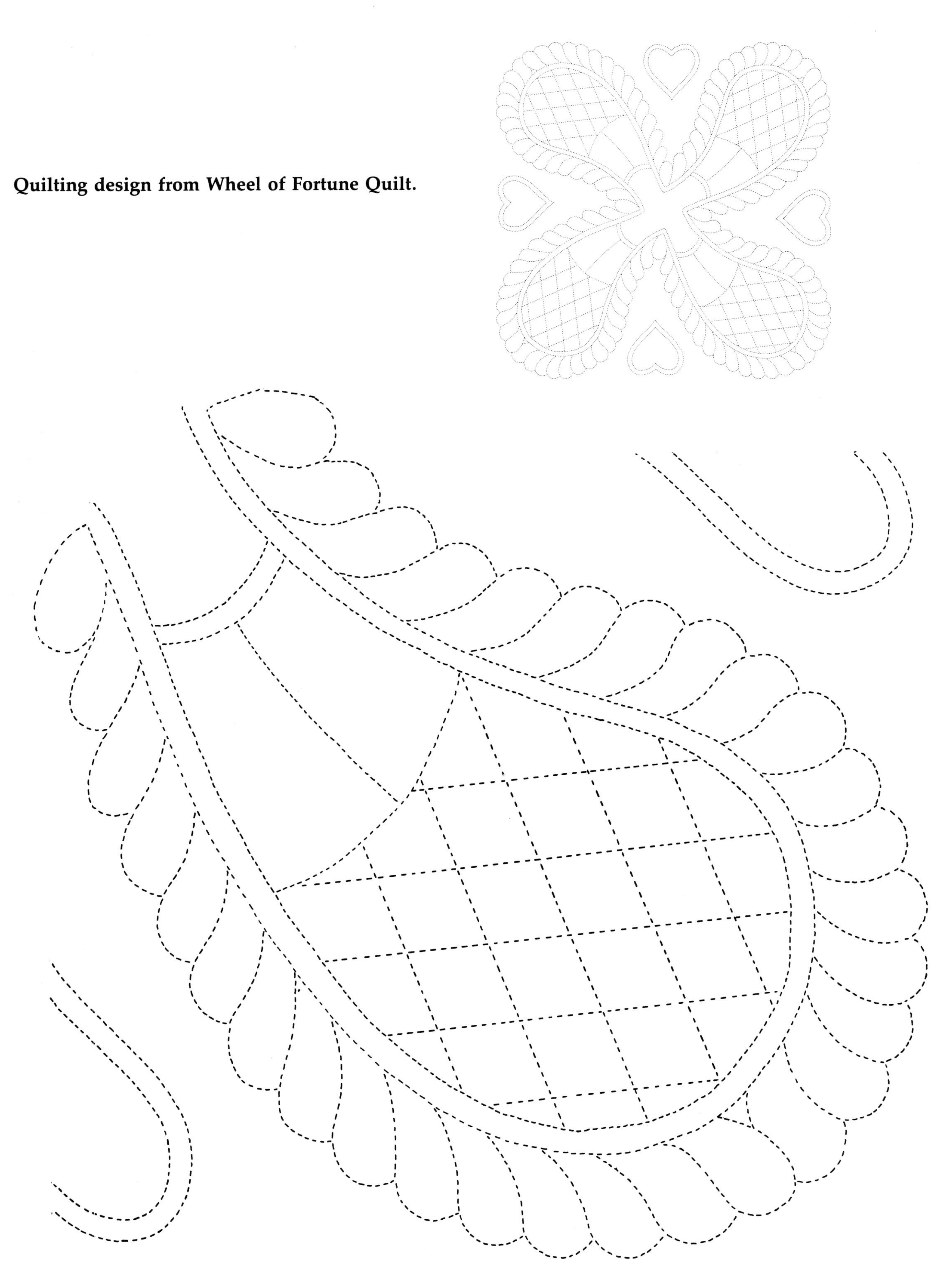

Quilting design from Victory Quilt.

Quilting design from Sunburst Quilt.